COOKING
FROM ABOVE
ITALIAN

COOKING FROM ABOVE

ITALIAN

LAURA ZAVAN

PHOTOGRAPHY BY PIERRE JAVELLE

✳ ✳ ✳

hamlyn

First published in France in 2007 under the title
Les basiques italiens, by Hachette Livre (Marabout)
Copyright © 2007 Hachette Livre (Marabout)

© Text Laura Zavan
Photography by Pierre Javelle

An Hachette UK Company
www.hachette.co.uk

First published in Great Britain in 2009 by
Hamlyn, a division of Octopus Publishing Group Ltd
2–4 Heron Quays, London E14 4JP
www.octopusbooksusa.com

Copyright © English edition
Octopus Publishing Group Ltd 2009

Distributed in the United States and Canada by
Hachette Book Group
237 Park Avenue, New York, NY 10017 USA

ISBN 978-0-600-61962-8

Printed and bound in Singapore

10 9 8 7 6 5 4 3 2 1

Measurements Standard level spoon measurements
are used in all recipes.

Nuts This book includes dishes made with nuts and
nut derivatives. It is advisable for those with known
allergic reactions to nuts and nut derivatives and
those who may be potentially vulnerable to these
allergies, such as pregnant and nursing mothers,
invalids, the elderly, babies, and children, to avoid
dishes made with nuts and nut oils. It is also advisable
to check the labels of preprepared ingredients for the
possible inclusion of nut derivatives.

Eggs should be large unless otherwise stated. The
Department of Health advises that eggs should not
be consumed raw. This book contains dishes made
with raw or lightly cooked eggs. It is advisable for
more vulnerable people, such as pregnant and nursing
mothers, invalids, the elderly, babies, and young
children, to avoid uncooked or lightly cooked dishes
made with eggs. Once prepared these dishes should
be kept refrigerated and used promptly.

Milk should be full fat unless otherwise stated.

Butter is unsalted unless otherwise stated.

Fresh herbs should be used unless otherwise stated.
If unavailable use dried herbs as an alternative but
halve the quantities stated.

Ovens should be preheated to the specific
temperature—if using a fan-assisted oven, follow
manufacturer's instructions for adjusting the time
and the temperature.

FOREWORD

~~~~~~

With this book you will discover, one step at a time, that Italian cookery is the most simple, tasty, and natural way of bringing food to the table that you could imagine… and one that is easily adapted to suit your requirements.

The recipes include a selection that are really quick to prepare and cook, such as the broiled vegetables or pasta dishes, and others that, even if you have never dared to attempt them before, such as risotto or homemade pizza, will no longer be a mystery to you! Some will give real pleasure, for example, making your own lasagne or ravioli—especially if you can prepare them with friends!

Italian cooking is founded on a simple philosophy: good ingredients. Think of a perfect tomato: its flavor, smell, texture, color. Served with no more than a drizzle of extra virgin olive oil and some basil: it's a feast!

It may take a little more time to seek out really good ingredients but once you've tracked down a decent source, everything becomes easy!

So allow yourself to discover this sun-filled cuisine, so warm and convivial. I invite you to share, like me, a moment of happiness: cooking is like love, and it does us so much good.

Buon appetito!

Laura

❋ ❋ ❋

CONTENTS

1
STARTERS

2
VEGETABLES

3
PASTA & CO.

4
FISH

5
MEAT

6
DESSERTS

APPENDICES
GLOSSARY • MENUS • TABLE OF CONTENTS
RECIPE INDEX • GENERAL INDEX
ACKNOWLEDGMENTS

STARTERS

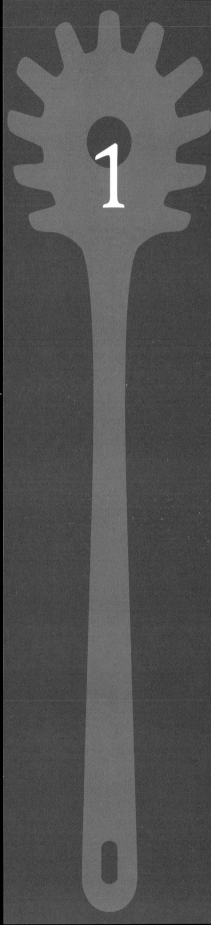

PESTOS

TOASTED

PIZZA & CO.

CLASSIC PESTO

⇢ SERVES 6 • PREPARATION: 15 MINUTES ⇠

6–8 handfuls of basil leaves (about 3½ oz)
¼ cup pine nuts
⅛ cup walnuts
1 garlic clove, peeled and crushed
salt flakes, pepper

¼ cup Parmesan, shredded
7 tablespoons olive oil

IN ADVANCE:
Clean the basil leaves. Put the bowl of a food-mixer, fitted with its blade, in the freezer for 1 hour. (This prevents the pesto from getting warm and losing its aromas.)

1 2
3 4

1	Dry-toast the pine nuts in a nonstick skillet, stirring them constantly. Remove from the heat and let cool.	2	Put the basil in the chilled bowl with the toasted pine nuts, walnuts, crushed garlic, and a pinch of salt and pepper.
3	Whiz for 30 seconds then add the shredded Parmesan and the oil, pouring it in as a thin stream.	4	The pesto is ready! Spread on toasted bread slices with some mozzarella, or stir into pasta, diluted with a little of its cooking water.

SICILIAN-STYLE PESTO

✣ **SERVES 6–8** • PREPARATION: 10 MINUTES ✣

Whiz together ⅓ cup each of: pitted black olives, pitted green olives, and sun-dried tomatoes with ¼ cup salted capers (rinsed), 1 tablespoon dried oregano, 1 handful of basil leaves, and 2 handfuls of flat leaf parsley. Pour in up to 7 tablespoons olive oil in a thin stream until the consistency is rich and smooth.

IDEAS:
Serve this pesto spread on toasted bread (bruschetta) or stirred into pasta, diluted with a little of its cooking water.

PISTACHIO PESTO

❖ SERVES 8 • PREPARATION: 10 MINUTES ❖

Toast 1 cup raw shelled pistachios for 10 minutes in the oven at 325°F. Let cool, then whiz with 3–4 handfuls of arugula leaves and ½ cup freshly shredded Pecorino romano. Pour in up to 10 tablespoons of olive oil in a thin stream until you have a smooth paste. Season with salt, pepper, and ground nutmeg.

IDEAS:

Serve this pesto spread on bruschetta, mixed with ricotta, or over pasta, or to accompany pan-fried or roasted meat.

SUNCHOKE PESTO

❖ SERVES 6–8 • PREPARATION: 30 MINUTES ❖

¼ cup almonds, skinned
6 tablespoons olive oil
2 garlic cloves
1 handful of flat leaf parsley

8 sunchoke hearts, fresh or frozen
salt
scant ⅓ cup freshly shredded Parmesan
4 tablespoons water

IN ADVANCE:
Lightly dry-toast the almonds in a skillet
then roughly chop them.

1 2
3 4

1	Heat 2 tablespoons of the olive oil in a skillet with 1 garlic clove and half the parsley.	2	Add the sunchoke hearts and brown on both sides over a high heat. Add salt and the water, cover, and simmer for 10 minutes.
3	Drain, let the hearts cool, then blend with the remaining garlic clove and parsley and the Parmesan. Pour in enough oil in a thin stream to make a smooth rich mixture.	4	It's ready! Serve the pesto spread on bruschetta or as an accompaniment to white meats.

BRUSCHETTA WITH TOMATO

❧ SERVES 4 • PREPARATION: 20 MINUTES • RESTING: 1 HOUR ❧

1 bunch of basil
1½ lb just-ripe plum tomatoes
7 tablespoons olive oil
3–4 garlic cloves, salt + pepper
8–10 slices of good-quality country-style bread, about ½-inch thick

IN ADVANCE:
Roughly chop the basil leaves. Skin the tomatoes (pierce with a knife then plunge in boiling water for 30 seconds and the skins will slip off easily).

VARIATIONS:
Instead of garlic on the bread, use anchovy fillets, marinated or in oil, or slices of buffalo mozzarella before topping with the tomatoes.

1 2
3 4

1	Deseed the tomatoes and cut into small dice. Put them in a colander and sprinkle with salt (this removes the excess water and accentuates their flavor). Set aside for 30 minutes.	2	Tip the tomatoes into a bowl with the olive oil, 2–3 garlic cloves, sliced (remove them before serving), and the basil. Taste and season as required. Set aside for a further 30 minutes.
3	Toast the bread slices, rub a cut garlic clove lightly over the surface, season, then drizzle with olive oil.	4	Top the bread slices with the diced marinated tomatoes and serve immediately.

BRUSCHETTA TOPPINGS

MEAT	CHEESE
✧ coppa (cured ham) + black olive tapenade	✧ warm Gorgonzola, mascarpone, + walnuts
✧ lardo di Colonnata (cured pork fat), tomato, + rosemary	✧ Pecorino + dried figs
✧ bresaola (air-dried salt beef), goats' cheese, + chives	✧ warm Taleggio + pan-fried zucchini
✧ prosciutto di San Daniele + sunchokes in oil	✧ smoked Provola, tomato, + arugula

BRUSCHETTA TOPPINGS

FISH OR SHELLFISH	VEGETABLES
⤙ Sicilian eggplants (see recipe 23) + steamed shrimp ⤙ broiled bell peppers (see recipe 16), tuna, + basil ⤙ canned mackerel in oil + tomato gratin (see recipe 25)	⤙ broiled vegetables (see recipes 16, 17, and 18) ⤙ botargo (salted grey mullet roe) marinated with celery stalks, lemon, + olive oil ⤙ oven-baked vegetables (see recipe 27) + capers

LINGUE

⇨ **MAKES 12** • PREPARATION: 30 MINUTES • COOKING: 10 MINUTES x 2 OR 4 BATCHES • RESTING: 2 HOURS ⇦

¼ oz fresh or ½ sachet dried yeast
7–10 tablespoons tepid water
¼ teaspoon sugar + 1 pinch
2 cups strong bread flour
½ teaspoon fine salt + olive oil

IN ADVANCE:
Prepare the dough following the method for pizza (see recipe 12) but using the quantities here. Work the dough for 5 minutes then let rise in a warm place, covered with a

kitchen towel, for 1 hour. Punch down, work again then let rise for a further 30 minutes. Preheat the oven to 475°F. Prepare a selection of toppings (see recipe 09 for some delicious ideas).

1 2
3 4

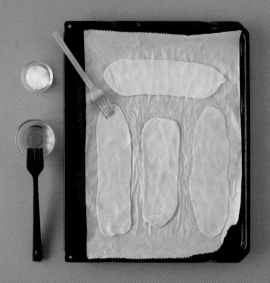
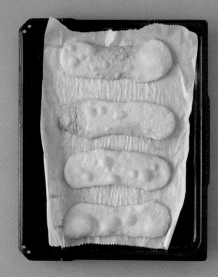

1	Take the prepared dough and form into 2 long sausage shapes a good inch in diameter then slice them into 12 even pieces.	2	Lightly dust a pastry board and rolling pin with flour and roll out each piece into rectangles measuring about 8 x 3 inches.
3	Arrange the rectangles on a baking sheet (or sheets) lined with baking paper. Brush them with oil, sprinkle with the salt, and prick them all over with a fork.	4	Sprinkle some water in the hot oven before baking the dough for 7–10 minutes or until the rectangles are golden-brown. If air pockets form in the dough, prick them with a needle.

BREADSTICKS (GRISSINI)

➔ **MAKES 30** • PREPARATION: 40 MINUTES • RESTING: 1 HOUR 30 MINUTES • COOKING: 15 MINUTES ◄

¾ oz fresh or 2 sachets dried yeast
¾–1 cup tepid water
½ teaspoon sugar + 1 pinch
4 cups strong bread flour
1 teaspoon fine salt + 6 tablespoons olive oil

IN ADVANCE:
Prepare the dough following the method for pizza (see recipe 12) but using the quantities here. Divide the dough into three pieces. Work a little dried oregano into the first,

1 tablespoon sesame seeds into the second, and 1 tablespoon chopped walnuts into the third. Let rise in a warm place, covered with a kitchen towel, for 1 hour.

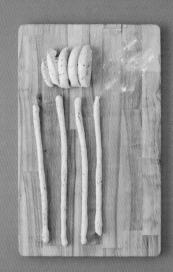

1 2
3 4

1	Lightly work each piece of dough for 30 seconds, then form into a sausage shape and cut into about 10 slices.	2	Use your hands to roll out each slice into sticks about ¾ inch thick and 4 inches long.
3	Arrange the breadsticks on a baking sheet lined with baking paper. Let rise for a further 30 minutes, covered with a damp kitchen towel.	4	Preheat the oven to 400°F and cook the breadsticks for about 15 minutes. See recipe 10 for serving ideas.

WHAT TO SERVE WITH LINGUE

TIP: SPREAD ONLY AT THE LAST MINUTE, OR SERVE THE TOPPINGS AND THE LINGUE SEPARATELY.

✧ ⅔ ricotta blended with ⅓ dried tomatoes + basil

✧ ⅔ ricotta blended with ⅓ Pistachio Pesto (recipe 03)

✧ ⅔ Pistachio Pesto blended with ⅓ botargo + pimiento

✧ ⅔ ricotta blended with ⅓ Pesto (recipe 01) + pine nuts

✧ Sicilian-style Pesto (recipe 02) + basil

✧ ½ mascarpone blended with ½ anchovies + oregano

✧ Sunchoke Pesto (recipe 04), parsley, + almonds

✧ tapenade + Oven-baked Cherry Tomatoes (recipe 26)

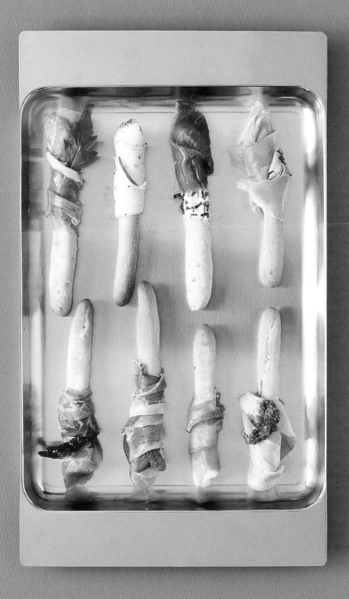

WHAT TO SERVE WITH GRISSINI

TIP: PREPARE ONLY AT THE LAST MINUTE SO THAT THE BREADSTICKS DON'T SOFTEN.

❧

- ✦ Parma ham, mascarpone, + arugula leaves
- ✦ lardo di Colonnata (cured pork fat), cut very finely
- ✦ bresaola, mascarpone, chives, + lemon rind
- ✦ cooked ham, sunchokes in oil + mascarpone

- ✦ coppa (cured ham), dried tomato paste, + mascarpone
- ✦ speck (cured mountain ham), butter, + dill pickles
- ✦ Culatello di Zibello (speciality Parma ham), on its own
- ✦ mortadella, Pistachio Pesto, + mascarpone

OLIVE FOCACCIA

✦ **SERVES 8** • PREPARATION: 30 MINUTES • RESTING: 2 HOURS 30 MINUTES • COOKING: 30 MINUTES ✦

Pizza dough (see recipe 12) made with
1½ cups water: it should be sticky
1 cup pitted taggiascha olives
6 tablespoons olive oil
4 tablespoons tepid water

1 level tablespoon salt flakes
VARIATIONS:
Work into the dough 2 tablespoons
chopped rosemary leaves, 1 small handful
snipped fresh sage leaves, or 10 salted

anchovy fillets, rinsed and cut very small.
Just before transferring the dough to
the oven, top with either 3½ oz halved
cherry tomatoes, or 2 onions sliced finely
into rings.

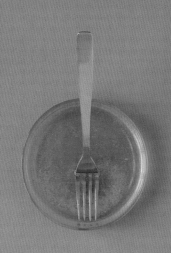

1 2
3 4

1	Work the dough, adding in the olives, for 1 minute before spreading it out on an oiled baking sheet, pressing it with your hands from the center toward the edge.	2	Use a fork to beat together the olive oil with the tepid water and the salt (the flakes should dissolve a little).
3	Using your fingertips, make little dimples over the surface of the dough, brush over half the oil mixture, and let rest for 30 minutes.	4	Preheat the oven to 350°F and cook the bread for 30 minutes until the top is golden. Brush with the remaining oil mix.

HOMEMADE PIZZA DOUGH

❧ PREPARATION: 20 MINUTES • RESTING: 2 HOURS 20 MINUTES • COOKING: 20 MINUTES ❧

1 oz fresh or 2 sachets of dried yeast
1–1¼ cups tepid water
½ teaspoon sugar + 1 pinch

4 cups strong bread flour
1 teaspoon fine salt
3 tablespoons olive oil

1 2
3 4

1	Crumble the yeast. Add 3 tablespoons of the water and the pinch of sugar. Leave for 15 minutes to activate.	2	Sift the flour into a large mixing bowl, sprinkle with the salt around the edges, then pour the yeast mixture into the center.	
3	Stir in the sugar and the oil, then gradually add in the remaining water.	4	Mix everything together using a fork.	➤

5 6
7 8

5	Work the dough for 5–10 minutes, adding a little extra water or flour as necessary.	6	The dough should be smooth and elastic. Form into a ball.
7	Put the dough into a large bowl, cut a cross into the surface using the tip of a knife, then cover with plastic wrap or a damp kitchen towel to prevent it drying out.	8	Let the dough prove for 1–2 hours; it should double in volume.

9

Punch down and work the dough for 1 minute then spread it out on an oiled baking sheet using your hands. For best results let rise again for a further 30 minutes, covered with a damp kitchen towel.

TIP

☞ For the yeast to work, the dough needs to rest in a warm place (77–86°F) away from any currents of air. Alternatively, place in an oven which has been preheated to 120°F and then switched off.

13

PIZZA MARGARITA

❧ **MAKES 10–14 SLICES** • PREPARATION: 30 MINUTES • RESTING: 2 HOURS • COOKING: 20 MINUTES ❧

1 quantity Pizza Dough (see recipe 12)
8 oz buffalo mozzarella (or, if you cannot find it, use a good mozzarella made from cow's milk)
14 oz canned chopped tomatoes

1 garlic clove, crushed
1 tablespoon dried oregano
about 10 basil leaves
3 tablespoons olive oil
salt

IN ADVANCE:
Rework the dough for 1 minute before spreading it out with your hands on an oiled baking sheet. If possible, rest it for 30 minutes, covered with a kitchen towel.

1 2
3 4

1	Cut the mozzarella into small dice then leave it to drain.	2	Put the tomatoes with the crushed garlic in a bowl with the oregano, half the basil, cut or torn into pieces, and 2 tablespoons olive oil. Add salt and taste to check the seasoning.
3	Spread this mixture over the dough and drizzle with the oil. Bake in a preheated oven at 475°F. Add the mozzarella after 12 minutes.	4	Cook for a further 6 minutes. The crust and the top should be golden. Serve with the remaining basil cut or torn and scattered on top.

PIZZA TOPPINGS

TO PIZZA MARGARITA (RECIPE 13) ADD ANY OF THE FOLLOWING TOPPINGS.

❧ **SALAMI:** once cooked, add some spicy salami.

❧ **EGGPLANTS:** 5 minutes before the end of cooking add some roasted or pan-fried eggplants (see recipes 17 and 24) and sprinkle with Parmesan.

❧ **MEDITERRANEAN:** at the end, add a few capers and black olives. Sprinkle with dried oregano.

❧ **SUMMER:** at the end, add cherry tomatoes marinated with garlic, basil, and olive oil, and some arugula leaves.

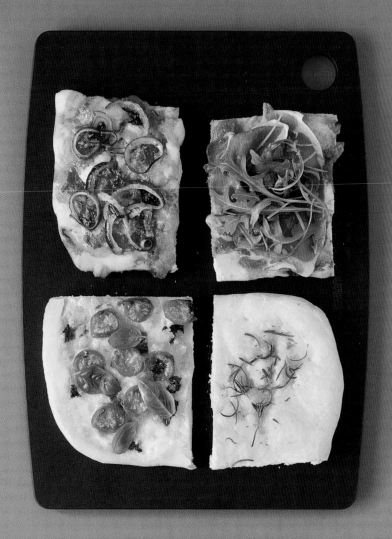

PIZZA TOPPINGS

TO PIZZA MARGARITA (RECIPE 13) ADD ANY OF THE FOLLOWING TOPPINGS.

✥ **ONION & ANCHOVY:** add 6 anchovies, some sliced onion, and olive oil before cooking.

✥ **'WHITE':** without tomato sauce. At the end, add cherry tomatoes, basil, and olive oil.

✥ **PARMA HAM & ARUGULA:** at the end, add some slices of Parma ham, arugula, and a drizzle of olive oil.

✥ **'WHITE' WITH ROSEMARY AND OLIVE OIL:** drizzle with olive oil and sprinkle with rosemary before cooking.

MINI FRIED CALZONE

❧ **MAKES 16** • PREPARATION AND COOKING: 1 HOUR ❧

8 oz mozzarella
about 10 basil leaves
1 quantity Pizza Dough (see recipe 12)
1½ cups Tomato Sauce (see recipe 40)

vegetable or olive oil, for deep-frying
IN ADVANCE:
Cut the mozzarella into small dice and leave
to drain. Roughly chop the basil.

IDEAS:
Add some chopped cured meats:
ham, salami, mortadella, and so forth.

1 2
3 4

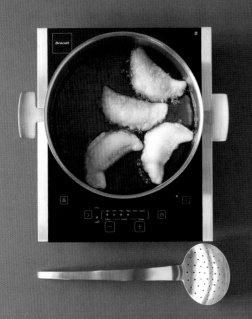

1	Form the dough into 4 pieces, then cut each one into 4 again. Flatten with your hand into 4-inch disks.	2	Mix the tomato sauce with the mozzarella and basil. Put about 1 teaspoon in the middle of each disk. Fold to enclose, pressing the edges.
3	Deep-fry immediately in plenty of hot oil until the dough is golden-brown on both sides. Do not overload the pan; cook in batches if need be.	4	Place the mini calzone on paper towels to absorb the excess oil then serve them hot.

VEGETABLES

2

BROILED VEGETABLES

SALADS

COOKED VEGETABLES

LIGHT DISHES

BROILED BELL PEPPERS

➤ **SERVES 4** • PREPARATION: 10 MINUTES • COOKING: 30 MINUTES • MARINATING: 1 HOUR ➤

4 bell peppers

FOR THE MARINADE:
olive oil
2–3 basil stalks (or other fresh herbs)
3 garlic cloves, thinly sliced
salt and freshly ground pepper

IN ADVANCE:
Preheat the broiler to its maximum setting.

1 2
3 4

1	Cut the peppers in half from top to bottom and remove the seeds and membranes. Place them in a baking tray, cut side down, under the broiler.	2	Watch them carefully: as soon as they develop dark patches, but without blackening completely, remove them from the broiler.
3	Place the peppers in a large bowl, cover it with plastic wrap, and let cool. Slip off the skins.	4	Cut the peppers into long thin slices then add the olive oil, basil, garlic, and some salt and pepper to the bowl. Marinate for 1 hour.

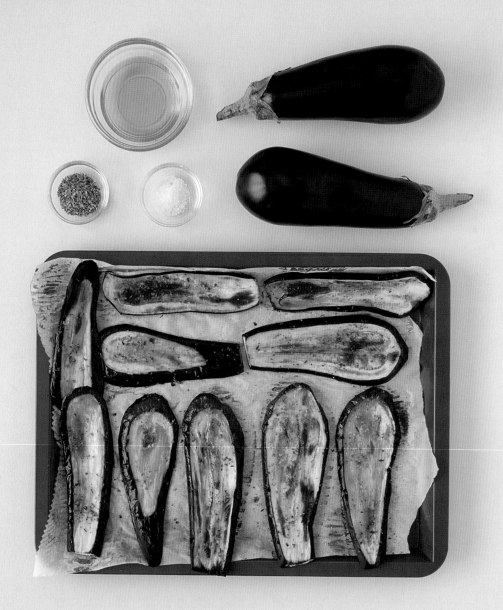

BROILED EGGPLANTS

✦ SERVES 4 • PREPARATION: 10 MINUTES • COOKING: 20 MINUTES ✦

Cut 2 eggplants lengthways into slices ¼ inch thick. Spread the slices out on a baking sheet covered with baking paper, brush with olive oil, and sprinkle with salt. Put under a very hot broiler until the slices are golden-brown (watch them carefully to make sure that they don't burn) then turn them over. Sprinkle with oregano and broil until the second side is golden.

BROILED ZUCCHINI

❧ SERVES 4 • PREPARATION: 10 MINUTES • COOKING: 20 MINUTES ❧

Cut 3 zucchini lengthways into slices ¼ inch thick. Spread them out in a baking tray covered with baking paper, brush with olive oil, and sprinkle with salt. Put under a very hot broiler until the slices are golden-brown (watch them carefully to make sure that they don't burn) then turn them over. Sprinkle with oregano and broil until the second side is golden. ☛ Dress the zucchini with vinegar, if liked.

ORANGE & FENNEL SALAD

⇾ SERVES 4 • PREPARATION: 20 MINUTES ⇽

2 large oranges
2 fennel bulbs
5–7 oz smoked swordfish (optional)
1 red onion

⅔ cup green olives
6 tablespoons olive oil
salt and freshly ground pepper

DELUXE VARIATION:
Instead of swordfish, you can use shavings of botargo.

1 2
3 4

1	Peel the oranges and cut the segements into pieces. Thinly slice the fennel and cut the swordfish (if using) into dice.	2	Slice the onion into rings and rinse in plenty of water to make the flavor less strong. Drain.
3	Combine the onion rings in a salad bowl with the oranges, fennel, swordfish, and olives.	4	Drizzle in the olive oil, season with salt and pepper, and it's ready!

PANZANELLA

⇝ **SERVES 4 • PREPARATION: 20 MINUTES • MARINATING: 1 HOUR** ⇜

8 slices of stale country-style bread
1 cup water
7 tablespoons olive oil + extra to serve
4 tablespoons good-quality red wine vinegar
salt and freshly ground pepper
1 red onion

1 lb cherry tomatoes
1 small cucumber, peeled and deseeded
2 celery stalks
¾ cup pitted black olives
⅓ cup salted capers, rinsed and chopped
1 bunch of basil

IN ADVANCE:
Put the bread slices in a salad bowl.

QUICK TIP:
If you don't have any stale bread, you can simply toast some fresh slices.

1   2   3
4   5   6

1	In a small bowl, mix together the water, olive oil, half the vinegar, and salt and pepper.	2	Pour this mixture over the bread and leave to swell. If there is not enough liquid, add a little extra water.	3	Cut the onion into rings and all the vegetables into even-sized dice. Transfer everything to a dish.
4	Add the olives, capers, basil, and the rest of the vinegar. Season with salt and pepper.	5	In a large salad bowl, layer alternately the soaked bread and the vegetables.	6	Leave to marinate for 1 hour. Drizzle with extra olive oil before serving.

RAW SUNCHOKE SALAD

⇝ SERVES 6 • PREPARATION: 15 MINUTES ⇜

6 small purple sunchokes (known as
poivrades or Provence sunchokes)
2 lemons
½ bunch of flat leaf parsley

6 tablespoons olive oil
salt flakes, freshly ground pepper
1 cup Parmesan shavings

SUGGESTION:
Serve with Carpaccio of Beef (see recipe
62) or with pan-fried Veal Escalopes (see
recipe 65).

1 2
3 4

1	Use a sharp knife to remove the top inch of the sunchokes and cut off their stalks. Remove the toughest outer leaves.	2	Put each prepared sunchoke immediately into water acidulated with some lemon juice to prevent them from blackening.
3	Cut the sunchokes into very thin slices. Chop the parsley.	4	Mix together the olive oil with 2 tablespoons of lemon juice and the parsley. Season with salt and pepper. Drizzle over the sunchokes and serve immediately, topped with the Parmesan.

STEWED PEPPERS (PEPERONATA)

❧ **SERVES 4** • PREPARATION: 15 MINUTES • COOKING: 35 MINUTES ❧

4 bell peppers (red, yellow, green)
4 ripe tomatoes, or use a can of chopped
tomatoes
2 onions

2 garlic cloves
3 tablespoons olive oil
1 bunch of basil
salt and freshly ground pepper

SUGGESTION:
This quintessentially summer dish can be
served with chicken, tuna, or rice dishes, or
spread on bruschetta.

1 2
3 4

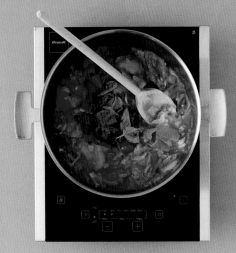

1	Deseed the bell peppers and cut into large chunks. Quarter and deseed the tomatoes. Finely chop the onions and the garlic.	2	Heat the oil in a pan and cook the onions for 2 minutes to soften. Add the tomatoes, bell peppers, garlic, and half the basil leaves.
3	Cook over a high heat for 5 minutes, add salt, then simmer, covered, for 20 minutes. Remove the lid and cook until the liquid has evaporated.	4	Roughly chop or tear the remaining basil leaves and stir in. Serve warm or at room temperature.

SICILIAN EGGPLANTS (CAPONATA)

➤ **SERVES 4–6** • PREPARATION: 30 MINUTES • COOKING: 20 MINUTES ◆

3 plum tomatoes
3 eggplants
2 celery stalks + 2 small onions
olive oil, for frying
4 tablespoons pitted green olives

1 tablespoon raisins
2 tablespoons pine nuts
1 tablespoon salted capers, rinsed
2 tablespoons red wine vinegar
1 level tablespoon sugar

IN ADVANCE:
Pierce the skins of the tomatoes then
plunge in boiling water for about
30 seconds. Refresh under running water
and slip off the skins.

1 2
3 4

1	Cut the eggplants into 1-inch cubes. String the celery and cut into small pieces. Quarter and deseed the tomatoes and dice. Finely chop the onions.	2	Heat the olive oil in a skillet and fry the eggplants, in batches, stirring frequently, until they are tender. (You may need to add extra oil between batches.) Season with salt.	
3	Drop the celery into boiling salted water for 2 minutes. Remove and drain.	4	Heat a little olive oil in another skillet, add the chopped onions, and cook for 2 minutes to soften.	➤

| 5 | Add the eggplants and the celery, then the olives, raisins, pine nuts, capers, and, at the end, the tomatoes. Gently stir to mix and let cook gently for 3 minutes. | **NOTE**
❋
☛ This is a lighter version of the original Sicilian caponata, which is made with deep-fried eggplants. |

| 6 | Mix together the vinegar and the sugar then pour into the skillet and continue to cook gently for a few minutes. | **SUGGESTION**
❋
Serve warm or at room temperature as a side dish, spread on bruschetta as a starter, or with a pasta salad or rice dish. |

NEAPOLITAN-STYLE EGGPLANTS

➤ **SERVES 4–6** • **PREPARATION: 30 MINUTES** • **COOKING: 25 MINUTES** ⦿

2 eggplants
2 oz Parmesan
4 oz mozzarella

1 bunch of basil
vegetable or olive oil, for deep-frying
salt
1 cup Tomato Sauce (see recipe 40)

TIP:
Have ready a good supply of paper towels
to absorb the excess oil from the eggplants.

1 2
3 4

1	Slice the eggplants thinly across their width.	2	Shred the Parmesan and chop the mozzarella and the basil leaves.
3	Heat the oil in a heavy-based, deep-sided casserole. Fry the eggplants in batches to avoid overcrowding the pan.	4	As soon as the slices are golden-brown, spread them on paper towels to absorb all the oil. Sprinkle lightly with salt. ➤

5

Grease a medium gratin dish and cover the base with a layer of eggplant slices. Top with some of the tomato sauce, sprinkle with chopped mozzarella, the basil, and shredded Parmesan. Repeat the layers until you have used up all the ingredients.

VARIATION
❊

☞ For a lighter version of this classic Neapolitan dish, melanzane alla parmigiana, you can broil the eggplant slices instead (see recipe 17).

| 6 | Transfer to a preheated oven at 350°F for about 5 minutes until the top is browned and bubbling. | **SERVING IDEAS**
❉
Serve warm or at room temperature as a starter, with a arugula salad, with rice, or as a side dish. |

TOMATO GRATIN

⊱ SERVES 4–6 • PREPARATION: 30 MINUTES • COOKING: 20 MINUTES ⊰

1 bunch of basil
½ bunch of flat leaf parsley
8 medium tomatoes
salt
4 tablespoons olive oil

4 anchovy fillets
1 garlic clove, cut in two
2 tablespoons dry oregano
⅔ cup freshly shredded Parmesan
1 cup homemade bread crumbs

IN ADVANCE:
Chop the basil and parsley.

1 2
3 4

1	Cut the tomatoes in half, remove the seeds and centers using a spoon, and sprinkle the insides with salt. Invert them on a board and let drain.	2	Heat a little oil in a pan and add the anchovies and garlic. Stir until the anchovies break down. Discard the garlic. Off the heat, mix in the herbs, Parmesan, bread crumbs, and half the oil.
3	Stuff the tomatoes with this mixture using 2 teaspoons then transfer them to a baking tray and drizzle with the remaining oil.	4	Cook in a preheated oven at 350°F for 20 minutes. Serve as a side dish.

OVEN-BAKED CHERRY TOMATOES

❧ **SERVES 4** • PREPARATION: 10 MINUTES • COOKING: 1 HOUR ❧

8 oz cherry tomatoes
olive oil
4 pinches of dry oregano (or use snipped
fresh basil leaves)

1 pinch of sugar
salt and freshly ground pepper

1	Cut the tomatoes in half and spread on a baking sheet covered with baking paper. Drizzle with olive oil and season with the oregano, sugar, and salt and pepper. Transfer to a preheated oven at 250°F and cook for 1 hour.

SERVING IDEAS
❋

Enjoy these tomatoes with mozzarella, in salads, with pasta and rice dishes, with meat, fish…

STORING
❋

☞ Store these tomatoes in a sealed tub in the fridge and use within 2–3 days.

OVEN-BAKED VEGETABLES

SERVES 4–6 • PREPARATION: 15 MINUTES • COOKING: 30 MINUTES

2 eggplants
1 red bell pepper
2 carrots
2 zucchini
1 fennel bulb

2 red onions
olive oil
salt and freshly ground pepper
1 tablespoon balsamic vinegar
1 bunch of basil or flat leaf parsley

IN ADVANCE:
Preheat the oven to 400°F.

1 2
3 4

1	Cut all the vegetables into even-sized chunks.	2	Place them in a baking pan large enough to accommodate them in a single layer. Season with olive oil, salt, and pepper.
3	Transfer to the preheated oven and cook for about 30 minutes, turning them 2 or 3 times.	4	Add the balsamic vinegar and snip the basil or parsley on top. Serve warm or at room temperature on bruschetta, with couscous or bulgar wheat salad, or as a side dish.

ZUCCHINI FRITTATA

→ **SERVES 6** • PREPARATION: 20 MINUTES • COOKING: 15 MINUTES ←

½ bunch of mint
½ bunch of basil
3 medium zucchini
2 tablespoons olive oil

1 garlic clove
salt and freshly ground pepper
12 eggs
½ cup freshly shredded Parmesan

IN ADVANCE:
Finely snip the herbs and cut the zucchini into rounds.

1 2
3 4

1	Heat a little oil in a skillet and add the garlic and zucchini. Cook, stirring, over a high heat for 5 minutes. Remove the garlic and season.	2	Briskly beat the eggs in a large bowl with a fork. Add the shredded Parmesan, the snipped herbs, and some salt and pepper.	
3	Pour the egg mixture over the zucchini then cook over a medium-high heat, shaking the pan frequently.	4	When the eggs start to set at the edges, bring them into the center using a wooden spoon.	➤

	As soon as the base is set, place a large plate over the skillet and quickly invert it. Add 1 tablespoon of olive oil to the skillet then slide the frittata back into the skillet to brown on the second side.	**VARIATION** ❋ You can use various vegetables in a frittata: pan-fried sunchokes, petits pois, asparagus tips, bell peppers, and so forth.
5		

		SERVING IDEAS
6	The frittata should be golden-brown on the outside and soft inside.	Serve hot, with a salad, or cold with an aperitif, cut into cubes.

HERB & VEGETABLE PIE

❧ **SERVES 6–8** • PREPARATION: 50 MINUTES • RESTING: 30 MINUTES • COOKING: 45 MINUTES ❧

PASTRY:
2 cups plain flour
3 tablespoons olive oil + 1 knob of butter
2 pinches of salt
7 tablespoons warm water

FILLING:
1¼ lb silverbeet, washed
1 lb frozen spinach, defrosted
olive oil + 4 tablespoons butter
3 oz smoked bacon or lardons

½ bunch of scallions with green parts
2 garlic cloves, chopped
salt, freshly ground pepper, and nutmeg
½ bunch of flat leaf parsley, chopped
¾ cup freshly shredded Parmesan

1 2
3 4

1	Mix together the flour and olive oil in a large mixing bowl. Incorporate the knob of butter by hand and add the salt.	2	Stir in enough water (add in stages) so that the mixture comes together to form a non-sticky ball.	
3	Turn out and work the dough for a few minutes on a board or counter top.	4	Cover with a clean kitchen towel and leave to rest for 30 minutes.	➤

5 6
7 8

5	Meanwhile, prepare the filling. Steam the silverbeet, allowing 7 minutes for the stalks and 5 minutes for the green leaves. Add the spinach at the end. Drain and let cool.	6	Heat 1 tablespoon olive oil in a skillet, add the smoked bacon (diced if using slices), and brown on all sides.
7	Add the chopped scallions (discard the tops of the greens) and garlic. Reduce the heat to very low and let cook for 5 minutes.	8	Use your hands to squeeze all the water from the silverbeet and spinach then chop them with a knife (not in a food-mixer!).

9 10
11 12

9	Add the chopped greens to the skillet and allow to dry for a few minutes, stirring. Season with salt, pepper, and 2–3 pinches of ground nutmeg.	10	Remove from the heat and let the mixture cool then add the chopped parsley and two-thirds of the Parmesan. Taste and adjust the seasoning as necessary.	
11	Flour your work surface and roll out half the pastry very thinly. Use it to line an oiled or nonstick baking tray.	12	Sprinkle the base with the remaining Parmesan then spread the cooked herbs and vegetables on top.	➢

13 Roll out the remaining pastry very finely and cover
the filling. Press the edges together to seal well then
prick the surface of the pie with the tines of a fork.

		SERVING IDEAS
14	Transfer to a preheated oven at 350°F and cook for 30 minutes. Brush the top of the pastry with olive oil and return the pie to the oven to brown.	☛ Allow the pie to cool then cut into portions and serve with salad, or cut into 16 small squares to serve as an aperitif.

MINESTRONE

❧ SERVES 6 • PREPARATION: 20 MINUTES • COOKING: 1 HOUR • SOAKING: 12 HOURS ☙

1¼ lb fresh shelled navy beans or 1 cup dry
navy beans
1 onion
2 celery stalks
2 carrots
2 potatoes

2 medium zucchini
2 silverbeet leaves (green parts only)
3½ oz French beans
3 tomatoes, skinned and deseeded
2 tablespoons chopped parsley
olive oil, salt and freshly ground pepper

IN ADVANCE:

If you are using dry beans, soak them in
cold water for 12 hours in advance. Rinse
and drain before adding with the vegetables.

1 2
3 4

1	Chop the onion and peel and cut all the other vegetables into even-sized pieces.	2	Heat 2 tablespoons of olive oil in a large stockpot. Add the onion, celery, and carrot and cook gently to soften.
3	Add the remaining vegetables, along with the navy beans. Season with salt and pour in enough water to cover.	4	Let simmer over a low heat for 1 hour. At the end of cooking, add the parsley, a drizzle of olive oil, and some freshly ground pepper.

BORLOTTI BEAN SOUP

➤ **SERVES 6** • PREPARATION: 15 MINUTES • COOKING: 3 HOURS • SOAKING: 12 HOURS ➤

1½ cups dry borlotti beans
1 pinch of baking soda or a 2-inch piece
of kombu
1 onion
1 garlic clove
1 celery stalk

1 carrot
7 tablespoons olive oil
1 oz cured pork fat or rind in the piece
1 rosemary stalk
1 bay leaf
salt and freshly ground pepper

10 cups water
3½ oz tagliatelle, broken in pieces
IN ADVANCE:
Soak the dry beans in cold water for
12 hours in advance with the baking soda
or the kombu. Rinse and drain.

1 2
3 4

1	Chop all the vegetables. Heat a little oil in a large stockpot and add all the vegetables with the pork fat, rosemary, and bay leaf. Season with salt.	2	Add the borlotti beans and 4 cups of water. Bring to a boil then reduce the heat and simmer for 2 hours, adding in extra boiling water as it cooks. Check the seasoning.
3	Blend half the soup in a blender or pass through a food mill.	4	Return the pot to the heat. When it boils, add the tagliatelle and cook until al dente. Serve the soup with a drizzle of olive oil and some pepper.

PASTA & CO.

EGG PASTA

SAUCES

HARD WHEAT PASTA

RISOTTO & GNOCCHI

HOMEMADE PASTA

❧ **MAKES 1 LB 10 OZ PASTA • PREPARATION: 30 MINUTES • RESTING: 1 HOUR** ❧

5 eggs
1–2 tablespoons milk
4 cups strong bread flour
1 pinch of salt
1 tablespoon olive oil

IN ADVANCE:
Take the eggs and milk from the fridge and bring to room temperature to ensure they mix evenly. Sift the flour with the salt on to a pastry board or counter top.

FOR LASAGNE VERDE:
Add ¾ cup cooked spinach, squeezed dry and blended, and use 3 eggs not 5 eggs in the recipe.

1 2
3 4

1	Make a well in the flour and break in the eggs. Mix with a fork.	2	Little by little, incorporate the flour using your fingertips.	
3	Use a spatula to bring in all the flour to make a dough. Work the dough on the board for 10 minutes using the palm of your hand. Add the milk, the olive oil, and a little more flour if necessary.	4	When the dough is smooth and shiny, shape into a ball, cover in plastic wrap, and let rest for between 30 minutes and up to 2 hours at room temperature.	➤

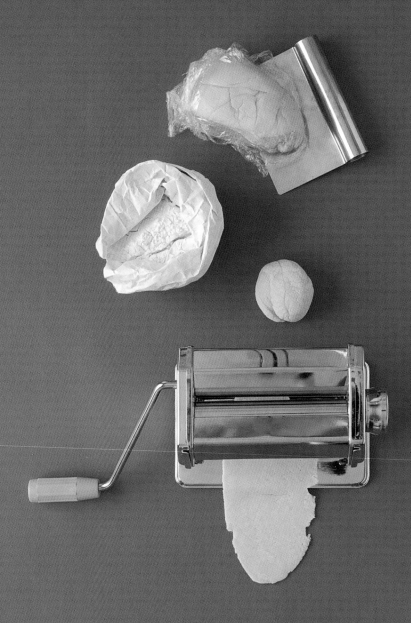

	TO ROLL OUT THE PASTA
	❋

| 5 | **WITH A PASTA MACHINE:** take about 2½ oz of the dough, flatten to a disc shape with the palm of your hand, lightly flour, then put through the machine with the rollers open to the maximum. | **BY HAND:** use a rolling pin, working always from the center to the edges. Work quickly to prevent the pasta from drying out. The thickness need not be exact but the more even it is, the better the sauce will cling to the pasta when it is cooked. |

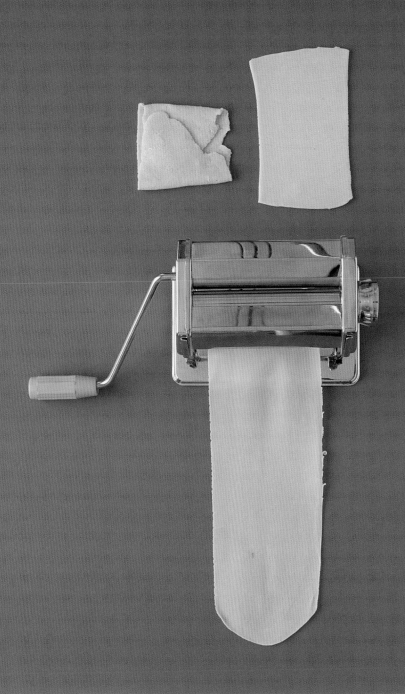

| 6 | Fold the dough in half or into thirds before putting it through the pasta machine to produce a thin sheet. Feed it through several times, each time tightening the rollers, until you have a thin, even sheet. | **TIP**
❋
Roll only a little dough at a time, keeping the remainder in a polythene bag so that it doesn't dry out. | ➢ |

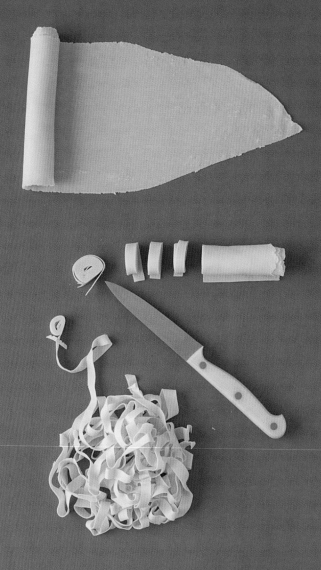

TO MAKE TAGLIATELLE

❋

7

Leave the sheets of pasta to dry out slightly (otherwise they will stick), then roll them up and cut them into ribbons ½ inch wide.

☛ Unroll the ribbons and arrange in a nest on a tray made of cardboard with holes in it (so that the air can circulate). Cover and keep them dry. Cook within 2 days.

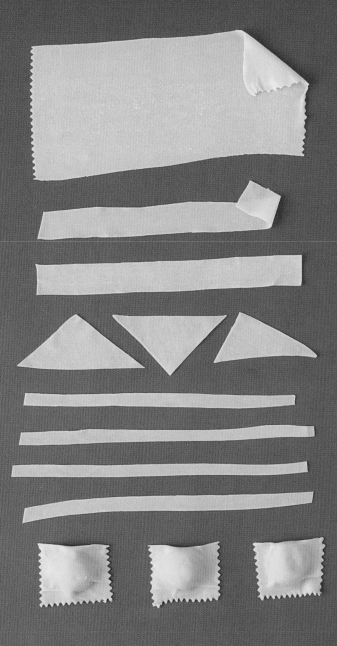

8

A 2½-oz block of dough makes lasagne sheets 4–5 inches wide and 16 inches long to trim according to your dish size. To make papardelle and tagliolini, follow the method for making tagliatelle but cut them into ribbons ¾ inch and ¼ inch wide respectively. Maltagliati are roughly cut pieces made from the trimmings.

TIP
※

☞ For a firmer pasta, use one-third semolina and two-thirds wheat flour, instead of all flour.

COOKING PASTA
※

Allow 4 cups of water and ½ teaspoon salt for every 3 oz of uncooked pasta.

PAPARDELLE WITH DUCK SAUCE

❧ **SERVES 6–8 • PREPARATION: 40 MINUTES • COOKING: 1 HOUR** ❧

DUCK SAUCE:
3½ oz carrots
3½ oz onions
3½ oz celery stalks
2 garlic cloves
1 duck, quartered

2 rosemary stalks
1 tablespoon olive oil
½ cup dry white wine
2 cups vegetable stock
14 oz canned tomatoes
salt and freshly ground pepper

1½ lb fresh papardelle (see recipe 32)
5 tablespoons butter
3½ oz Parmesan
IN ADVANCE:
Finely chop the vegetables.

1 2
3 4

1	Brown the duck on all sides, skin-side down first, in a little of the olive oil. Discard the fat and place the duck in a Dutch oven.	2	Heat the remaining oil in a skillet, add all the vegetables and the rosemary, and cook for 5 minutes, stirring frequently.
3	Put everything in the Dutch oven with the duck over a high heat. As soon as it is hot, pour in the wine and let evaporate.	4	Stir in the stock and tomatoes. Season with salt and pepper. Cover and leave to cook over a gentle heat for 45 minutes. ➤

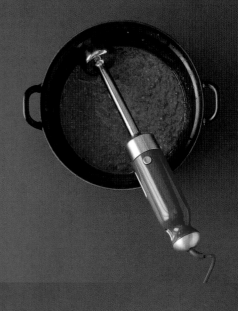

5 6
7 8

5	When the duck is cooked, let cool slightly then remove the skin and bones and cut the meat into small pieces.	6	If the sauce is too liquid, allow to reduce then blend it smooth with a stick blender. Remove any fat that collects on the surface with a spoon.
7	Return the duck meat to the Dutch oven and gently reheat for 5 minutes.	8	Meanwhile cook the pasta in boiling salted water for 3–4 minutes after it has come back to the boil. Drain, return to the pan, and mix in the butter.

9	Top the pasta with the duck sauce and serve with the shredded Parmesan.

VARIATION
❀

This sauce can also be used to make a lasagne, layered with a little Béchamel Sauce (see recipe 35).

TIP
❀

☛ If possible, prepare the duck sauce the day before. When cooled, the fat will solidify, making it easier to remove from the surface.

TAGLIATELLE WITH MUSHROOMS

✦ **SERVES 4** • PREPARATION: 45 MINUTES • COOKING: 30 MINUTES ✦

MUSHROOM SAUCE:
1¼ lb mixed wild mushrooms (ceps,
girolles, oyster, and so forth)
2 tablespoons olive oil + 2 knobs butter
salt and freshly ground pepper

2 garlic cloves
½ bunch of flat leaf parsley
1 lb fresh tagliatelle (see recipe 32)
¼ cup freshly shredded Parmesan

IN ADVANCE:
Clean the mushrooms, scraping them with a
knife to remove the soil. Plunge them twice
into water, remove immediately, and wipe dry.

1	Cut the biggest mushrooms in half or thirds then spread them out to dry on a clean kitchen towel.	2	Heat the oil with the 2 knobs of butter and the garlic. Add the mushrooms and cook over a high heat to release their water. Do not stir.
3	Season with salt and pepper, add a little chopped parsley, and let cook for a further 3 minutes over a gentle heat (discard the garlic). Keep warm.	4	Cook the tagliatelle until al dente. Put a little of the cooking water into a skillet, melt the butter, then stir in the drained tagliatelle, the mushrooms, and the Parmesan.

BÉCHAMEL SAUCE

❖ **ENOUGH TO MAKE 1 LASAGNE** • PREPARATION: 10 MINUTES • COOKING: 15 MINUTES ❖

6 tablespoons butter
⅔ cup all-purpose flour
4 cups milk

4 pinches freshly ground nutmeg
salt

1
4

2
5

3
6

1	Melt the butter in a small pan over a gentle heat.	2	Sprinkle the flour over the top, stirring with a whisk.	3	When the mixture starts to take on color, gradually add the milk.
4	Stir constantly to prevent any lumps forming.	5	Leave to cook gently for 10 minutes. Add the nutmeg and salt.	6	Let cool; if the sauce seems too thick, stir in a little more milk.

LASAGNE VERDE BOLOGNAISE

❧ **SERVES 6** • PREPARATION: 1 HOUR 30 MINUTES • COOKING: 1 HOUR 30 MINUTES – 2 HOURS ❧

1 oz dry ceps (wild mushrooms)
3½ oz carrots
3½ oz onions
3½ oz celery stalks
3 tablespoons olive oil
12 oz braising beef, cubed small

12 oz shoulder of veal, cubed small
⅔ cup red wine
salt and pepper
1 cup vegetable bouillon
fresh herbs, tied as a bouquet garni
2 cloves

14 oz canned tomatoes
8–12 spinach lasagne sheets (see recipe 32)
2 tablespoons butter
Béchamel Sauce (see recipe 35)
5 oz Parmesan

1 2
3 4

1	Soak the dry mushrooms for 30 minutes in 1 cup of warm water. Strain the soaking water and reserve.	2	Finely chop all the vegetables.	
3	Heat the oil in a Dutch oven, add the meat and all the chopped vegetables, and cook over a high heat, stirring, for 20–30 minutes.	4	When the mixture starts to catch on the base of the oven, pour in the wine. Allow the liquid to evaporate.	➤

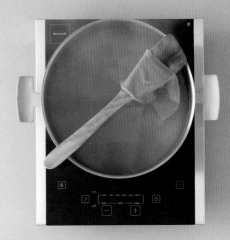

5 6
7 8

5	Season with salt, add the mushrooms, soaking water, stock, herbs, and cloves. Simmer for 1 hour, adding the tomatoes midway through.	6	To cook the lasagne, lower the sheets, 3 or 4 at a time, into a large pan of boiling salted water with a little olive oil. Cook for 2–3 minutes.
7	Immediately put the sheets in a bowl of cold water to stop the cooking, drain, then spread them out on a clean kitchen towel without any overlapping.	8	Butter a gratin dish, pour a little béchamel into the base, then build up alternate layers of lasagne, béchamel, and bolognaise sauce, sprinkling Parmesan on each layer.

9	Continue to build up layers, ending with one of béchamel mixed with 4 tablespoons of the bolognaise sauce. Sprinkle with Parmesan and dot with butter. Transfer to the oven preheated to 350°F for 30 minutes. Remove from the oven and let rest for 5 minutes before cutting into portions. Buon appetito!

TIP
※

☛ You can of course make this dish with plain lasagne. It's best to precook the sheets in advance.

VARIATION
※

Serve tagliatelle with this bolognaise sauce, as they do in Emilia Romagna.

ASPARAGUS & PEA LASAGNE

❖ **SERVES 6** • PREPARATION: 40 MINUTES • COOKING: 50 MINUTES ❖

2 lb fresh peas in the pod or 2 cups
shelled peas
1 bunch of green asparagus spears
1 bunch of early crop onions or scallions
2–3 tablespoons olive oil

3–4 knobs of butter
salt
8–12 lasagne sheets (see recipe 32)
Béchamel Sauce (see recipe 35)
1 lb burrata or ricotta

1 cup Parmesan
ground nutmeg

IN ADVANCE:
Shell the peas.

1	Cut the green of the asparagus stalks (not the woody parts) into small rounds and cut the onions, including the green parts, into dice.	2	Heat a little oil and a knob of butter in a skillet. Sauté the asparagus rounds and onion separately (they should retain a little bite). Season with salt.
3	Bring a small pan of salted water to a boil, drop in the asparagus tips, and boil for 2–3 minutes, drain, then set aside.	4	Cook the shelled peas over a gentle heat in a little salted water until tender. ➤

5 6
7 8

5	To cook the lasagne, lower the sheets, 3 or 4 at a time, into a large pan of boiling salted water with a little olive oil. Cook for 2–3 minutes.	6	Immediately put the sheets in a bowl of cold water to stop the cooking, drain, then spread them out on a clean kitchen towel without any overlapping.
7	Butter a gratin dish and build up alternate layers of lasagne, béchamel, vegetables, and crumbled cheese. Sprinkle with Parmesan.	8	Continue to build up a further 2 sets of layers, ending with lasagne then crumbled cheese and a sprinkling of Parmesan.

9 Transfer to the oven preheated to 350°F for 20 minutes until browned and bubbling. Just before serving, melt a knob of butter in a skillet. Toss the reserved asparagus tips in the butter and use to garnish the lasagne.

VARIATION
❋

Mix these vegetables with tagliatelle and stir in some melted butter with a little of the pasta cooking water.

TIP
❋

☛ If you don't have time to make your own pasta, buy good-quality dried lasagne sheets made with eggs, which you will find in Italian delicatessens.

SPINACH & RICOTTA CRÊPES

❖ SERVES 6 • PREPARATION: 1 HOUR • RESTING: 1 HOUR • COOKING: 1 HOUR ❖

CRÊPE BATTER:
1 cup all-purpose flour
3 eggs
salt
1½ tablespoons melted butter
1 cup milk

FILLING:
1¼ lb fresh or 10 oz frozen spinach
1 tablespoon olive oil + 4 tablespoons butter
1 garlic clove, cut in half
salt and freshly ground pepper

few pinches of ground nutmeg
1 cup ricotta + ½ cup mascarpone
2 tablespoons bread crumbs
¾ cup freshly shredded Parmesan
IN ADVANCE:
Steam the spinach, drain, and squeeze dry.

1 2
3 4

1	First make the batter. Put the flour in a mixing bowl and make a well in the center. Add the eggs, salt, and melted butter. Beat together.	2	Stir in the milk, beating constantly to avoid any lumps. Cover the bowl with plastic wrap and let rest for 1 hour.	
3	Heat a skillet with the oil, half the butter, and the garlic. Dry the spinach over a medium heat. Season with salt, pepper, and nutmeg.	4	Put in a bowl to cool. Add the ricotta, mascarpone, bread crumbs, and two-thirds of the Parmesan. Check the seasoning.	➤

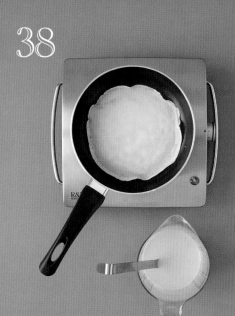

5 6
7 8

5	Make the crêpes in a small nonstick skillet brushed with a little butter between each one. Keep them small and thin (you should get 12–14 in all), discarding the first.	6	Form a sausage shape of filling on each crêpe (use about 3–4 tablespoons for each one) and roll up tightly.
7	Cut each roll into four.	8	Butter a gratin dish and pack in the crêpes, end-up. Sprinkle with the remaining Parmesan and dots of butter.

| 9 | Brown in a preheated oven at 400°F. It's ready! | **VARIATION**
❋

These crêpes can be used to replace lasagne sheets. You can stuff them with Bolognaise Sauce (see recipe 36), with a little Béchamel Sauce (see recipe 35), or with vegetables such as asparagus or peas (see recipe 37). |

RAVIOLI STUFFED WITH SQUASH

⟩ **SERVES 10** • PREPARATION: 1 HOUR • COOKING: 50 MINUTES ⟨

FILLING:
6 tablespoons apple condiment or
5 tablespoons Mostarda di Cremona
2 oz amaretti di Saronno
2 lb squash (acorn, kabocha, etc)

3 pinches ground nutmeg
2 pinches cinnamon
1 cup freshly shredded Parmesan
salt and white pepper
1 lb 10 oz Homemade Pasta (see recipe 32)

knob of butter per person
12 sage leaves
IN ADVANCE:
Blend the mostarda to a smooth purée.
Crush the amaretti.

1 2
3 4

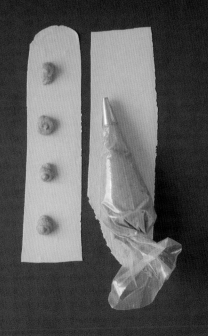

1	Cut up the squash and remove the seeds and fibers. Bake in a preheated oven at 350°F for 40 minutes until tender.	2	Blend the cooked squash, then add the spices, amaretti, mostarda, half the Parmesan, and salt and pepper.
3	Roll out the pasta into very thin sheets. Use a piping bag (or a teaspoon), to make regularly spaced (2 inches apart) little heaps of stuffing in the middle of the pasta.	4	Fold over the pasta to enclose the filling. Press around the filling with your fingers to seal each one and remove air pockets. Use a ravioli cutter to make parcels.

| 5 | Cook the ravioli, 3 or 4 portions at a time, in a large pan of lightly salted simmering water for about 3 minutes. Remove, drain, and place in serving bowls with a helping of sage butter (see opposite) on each portion. | **SAGE BUTTER**
❊

Melt a knob of butter per person over a gentle heat with the sage leaves and a little water. |

6	Serve hot, with freshly shredded Parmesan.	**TIP** ☞ If the pasta has dried a little, brush the edges with a wash of egg white and a little water.
PREPARATION IN ADVANCE		**VARIATIONS**
☞ You can make your ravioli the day before and keep them, covered, on a tray in the fridge, between two clean kitchen towels, or freeze them spread out flat.		Use the spinach and ricotta filling (see recipe 38) or shredded cheese (5 oz ricotta, 7 oz mild Pecorino, and 4 oz Parmesan) and 1 egg.

TOMATO SAUCE

SERVES 4–6 • PREPARATION: 15 MINUTES • COOKING: 30 MINUTES

1 onion	2 lb ripe plum tomatoes or	handful of basil
1 carrot	1 lb 10 oz canned chopped tomatoes	salt
1 celery stalk	2 tablespoons olive oil	

1 2
3 4

1	Finely chop the onion, carrot, and celery. If you are using fresh tomatoes, cut into quarters, remove the seeds, and cut the flesh into pieces.	2	Heat the olive oil in a pan, add the vegetables, and cook for 10 minutes until softened. Add the tomatoes, half the basil, and a little salt.
3	Cook over a high heat for 2 minutes then for 15 minutes over a medium heat, stirring regularly. Pass through a food mill.	4	Add the remaining basil. The sauce will keep in the fridge for 2–3 days in a clean pickles jar covered with a layer of olive oil.

ANCHOVY & GARLIC SAUCE

❖ **FOR 8 OZ OF PASTA** • PREPARATION: 10 MINUTES • COOKING: 20 MINUTES ❖

Heat 2 tablespoons of olive oil in a skillet and soften 3 anchovy fillets. Add 1 garlic clove and 1 tablespoon of rinsed, chopped capers. Stir for 1 minute then add the chopped tomatoes, 2 pinches of chili powder, and ½ cup of pitted black olives, cut into rounds. Cook for 2 minutes over a high heat then for 8–10 minutes over a medium heat, stirring often. At the end, add salt and 2 tablespoons chopped flat leaf parsley. (Note: there is no cheese in this version; it doesn't go well with fish!)

CHILE & BACON SAUCE

⤞ FOR 8 OZ OF PASTA • PREPARATION: 10 MINUTES • COOKING: 20 MINUTES ⤝

Heat 2 tablespoons of olive oil in a skillet and soften 1 chopped onion and 3 oz of pancetta cut into small dice. Add the chopped tomatoes and 2 pinches of chili powder. Cook over a high heat for 2 minutes then for a further 8–10 minutes over a medium heat, stirring often. At the end, add salt to taste and generous amounts of ground pepper and sprinkle with freshly shredded Pecorino or Parmesan.

CARBONARA WITH SUNCHOKES

❧ **SERVES 4** • PREPARATION: 30 MINUTES • COOKING: 20 MINUTES ❧

4 tablespoons olive oil
4 small purple sunchokes (poivrades)
1 garlic clove
1 tablespoon chopped flat leaf parsley
½ glass white wine or vegetable bouillon

salt and freshly ground pepper
12 oz spaghettoni (large spaghetti)
4 oz fatty pancetta or lardons
1 whole egg + 3 egg yolks
¾ cup freshly shredded Parmesan

IN ADVANCE:
Prepare the sunchokes and cut them into fine slices (see recipe 21). Cut the pancetta into dice.

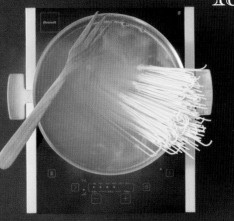

1 2
3 4

1	Heat 2 tablespoons of the oil and cook the sunchokes with the garlic and parsley. Add the wine and let it evaporate. Season with salt and pepper. The sunchokes should retain some bite.	2	Cook the pasta in a large pan of boiling salted water until al dente.	
3	Heat a little oil in a second skillet and brown the pancetta on all sides.	4	Mix the eggs with the Parmesan, a little more oil, and salt and pepper. Moisten with a little of the pasta cooking water.	➢

5 | Put the drained pasta in a large bowl with
2 or 3 tablespoons olive oil and the pancetta.
Add in the egg mixture and the sunchokes.
Combine thoroughly.

| 6 | Grind plenty of pepper on top and serve immediately. | **TRADITIONAL CARBONARA**
❋
☛ In Italy spaghetti alla carbonara was traditionally prepared with salted pork cheek instead of pancetta, and without sunchokes or creamy sauce! |

PENNE WITH EGGPLANTS

❧ SERVES 4 • PREPARATION: 20 MINUTES • COOKING: 20 MINUTES ❧

2 eggplants
4 tablespoons olive oil
1 garlic clove
2 cups Tomato Sauce (see recipe 40)
handful of basil

3 cups penne
½ cup fresh or salted ricotta, crumbled
2 oz Pecorino or Parmesan, shredded
freshly ground pepper

IN ADVANCE:
Cut the eggplants into cubes.

1 2
3 4

1	Heat a skillet with 2 tablespoons olive oil and the garlic then add some of the eggplants (cook in batches, not to overcrowd the pan).	2	Cook the eggplants over a gentle heat, stirring often, until they are soft and colored. Return all the cooked eggplants to the pan at the end.
3	Add the tomato sauce and half the basil. Let bubble gently for a few minutes.	4	Cook the pasta until al dente, drain, then mix with the sauce. Serve garnished with the ricotta, Pecorino, pepper, and the remaining basil.

BUCATINI WITH FRESH SARDINES

➤ **SERVES 4** • PREPARATION: 30 MINUTES • COOKING: 50 MINUTES ◄

8–10 fresh whole sardines + 4 to garnish
2 tablespoons small raisins
1 fennel bulb + 1 teaspoon fennel seeds
olive oil
1 large onion, finely chopped

5 tablespoons pine nuts
2 pinches powdered saffron or a few threads
2 anchovy fillets, rinsed and chopped
salt and freshly ground pepper
1 lb bucatini (thick spaghetti)

IN ADVANCE:
Clean the sardines and remove the head
and backbone to give 2 fillets (see recipe
61). Soak the raisins for 15 minutes in
warm water.

1 2
3 4

1	Bring 3½ quarts of water to a boil. Add the fennel, cut in half, and the seeds. Cook for 15 minutes then drain, reserving the water.	2	Heat 1 tablespoon of olive oil. Add the onion, soften for 2 minutes, then add 1 glass of the fennel cooking water. Allow to reduce by half.
3	Add 4 more tablespoons of oil and the raisins, pine nuts, saffron, and fennel. Let simmer for 5 minutes.	4	Add the sardines (reserving 4 as garnish) and the anchovies. Lightly season with salt and pepper and cook for a further 5 minutes, stirring, over a gentle heat. ➤

5	Heat a little olive oil in a skillet and fry the remaining 4 sardines on both sides until they start to color. (You can dust them first with a little flour if you wish.) Remove the sardines and keep warm.

COOKING THE PASTA
❊

Bring the reserved fennel cooking water to a boil in a large pan (topped up with fresh water if necessary), add some salt and cook the pasta until al dente. Drain thoroughly.

6

Sauté the pasta in the oil in which you fried the 4 sardines then add the sauce and the rest of the sardines. Garnish the dish with the reserved fried sardines and serve.

GRATIN VERSION
❋

Prepare the sauce using all the sardines. Cook then drain the pasta and dress with oil. In a large oiled gratin dish, alternate layers of pasta and sauce, ending with a layer of sauce. Top with bread crumbs and pine nuts then put in the oven to brown before serving.

LINGUINE WITH CLAMS

⟶ SERVES 2 • PREPARATION: 40 MINUTES • COOKING: 30 MINUTES ⟵

1 lb clams, in the shell
1–2 tablespoons olive oil
2 garlic cloves
½ bunch of flat leaf parsley, chopped

few pinches mild chili flakes
½ cup dry white wine
salt and freshly ground pepper
7 oz linguine or spaghetti

IN ADVANCE:
Carefully wash the clams in plenty of cold running water. Discard any with shells that remain open.

1 2
3 4

1	Heat the oil in a Dutch oven. Add 1 halved garlic clove, one-third of the parsley, and 1 pinch of chili. Cook for 1 minute then add the wine.	2	Wait for 1 minute after the wine has come to a boil then add the clams.	
3	Cover the pan and allow to boil just until all the clam shells are open. Remove the clams with a slotted spoon and let them cool in a colander over a bowl.	4	Strain the cooking water through a fine-mesh strainer. Reserve a quarter of the clams in their shells as garnish and shell the remainder.	➤

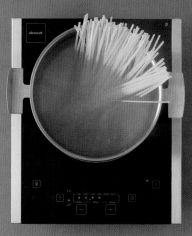

5 6
7 8

5	Heat 1 tablespoon of oil and add the second garlic clove (then remove and discard it), the remaining chili, 2 pinches of parsley, and the clam cooking water. Let reduce then add salt.	6	Meanwhile bring a large pan of salted water to a boil and cook the linguine until al dente.
7	Just before the pasta is cooked, add the shelled clams to their cooking juices.	8	Drain the linguine and toss in the pan with the clams and 2 tablespoons of olive oil.

9

Serve hot, with a good grinding of pepper, the remaining chopped parsley, and the reserved clams in their shells as garnish.

VARIATION
❄

All or a portion of the clams may be replaced by mussels (preparation and cooking steps are identical).

PASTA GRATIN

❧ SERVES 6 • PREPARATION: 30 MINUTES • COOKING: 20 MINUTES ❧

1 lb paccheri (large tube pasta)
8 oz mozzarella
5 oz smoked Provola
3½ oz Parmesan
2½ cups Tomato Sauce (see recipe 40)

handful of basil
1½ tablespoons butter
4–6 tablespoons bread crumbs
1 cup ricotta
salt and freshly ground pepper

IN ADVANCE:
Bring a large pan of salted water to a boil then cook the pasta until al dente. Drain.

1 2
3 4

1	Cut the mozzarella and the Provola into small pieces and shred the Parmesan.	2	Mix the cooked pasta with the tomato sauce, half the Parmesan, and some basil leaves.
3	Butter a gratin dish, sprinkle the base with bread crumbs, pour in half the pasta mixture and cover with half the mozzarella, Provola, and crumbled ricotta. Top with the remaining basil then repeat the pasta and cheese layers.	4	Sprinkle with bread crumbs and the remaining Parmesan and dot with butter. Season with salt and pepper. Put in a preheated oven at 350°F for about 20 minutes until the top is crisp and golden-brown.

SICILIAN-STYLE PASTA SALAD

➤ **SERVES 6** • PREPARATION: 10 MINUTES • COOKING: 8 MINUTES ←

8 oz cherry tomatoes
salt and freshly ground pepper
½ cup mi-cuit tomatoes in olive oil
½ cup pitted black taggiasca olives

2 tablespoons salted capers, rinsed
extra virgin olive oil
2 tablespoons dry oregano
3 cups penne or pennoni

7 oz loin of tuna (or white tuna) preserved
in olive oil

1 2
3 4

1	Cut the cherry tomatoes in half and sprinkle with salt. Roughly chop the mi-cuit tomatoes, the olives, and the capers.	2	Mix all these ingredients with 4 tablespoons of the olive oil, the oregano, salt, and pepper.
3	Cook the pasta until al dente, then drain and rinse immediately under cold running water to stop the cooking. Spread out on a baking tray and drizzle with oil to stop them sticking.	4	Combine the pasta with the vegetables. Add the tuna, separated into large chunks, and more olive oil, if necessary. Taste and adjust the seasoning.

PASTA STUFFED WITH VEGETABLES

➤ **SERVES 4–6** • PREPARATION: 30 MINUTES • COOKING: 30 MINUTES ◄

2 eggplants
2 medium zucchini
2 bell peppers of different colors
2 garlic cloves

salt
4–5 tablespoons olive oil
1 lb conchiglioni (or other large pasta)
6 tablespoons Classic Pesto (see recipe 01)

1 2
3 4

1	Wash the vegetables and cut them all into small dice.	2	Cook them separately in 1 tablespoon of oil with 1 garlic clove (remove at the end), and salt. The zucchini and peppers should retain a little bite; the eggplants should be soft.	
3	Place all the cooked vegetables in the same skillet and allow them to gently cook for a few minutes.	4	Cook the pasta until al dente, drain, and immediately rinse under cold running water. Spread on a sheet and oil them.	➢

5

Put a small spoonful of the pesto in each pasta shell then fill with 1 tablespoon of vegetables.

VARIATION
❋

Stuff the pasta with 1 tablespoon of Caponata (see recipe 23) or with 2 teaspoons ricotta mixed with 1 teaspoon Classic Pesto (see recipe 01) or Pistachio Pesto (see recipe 03). You can also mix the pasta with the vegetables and pesto as a salad.

6	It's ready!	
		This dish is best served at room temperature, either as something to nibble with drinks or as a summer starter.
	GARNISH ❊	
	You can garnish the shells with a basil leaf, a few grilled pine nuts, or shavings of Parmesan.	

CLASSIC RISOTTO

❖ SERVES 4 • PREPARATION: 10 MINUTES • COOKING: 25 MINUTES ❖

5 cups meat or vegetable bouillon
1 onion
1 tablespoon olive oil + 1 tablespoon butter
1½ cups risotto rice (carnaroli, arborio, or vialone nano)

salt
¼ cup dry white wine (or extra bouillon)
⅓ cup freshly shredded Parmesan, and a few shavings to garnish
3 tablespoons cold butter, cubed

IN ADVANCE:
Heat the bouillon and keep it at a gentle simmer. Finely chop the onion.

| 1 2 |
| 3 4 |

1	Heat the oil and 1 tablepoon of the butter in a heavy-based saucepan. Add the onion and cook gently for 5 minutes to soften.	2	Turn up the heat and add the rice (no need to wash it). Stir for 2 minutes until the grains are translucent but not colored. Season with salt, add the wine, and stir until it is all absorbed.	
3	Pour in 1 ladleful of hot bouillon and cook over a medium heat for 15 minutes. Keep adding a ladle of bouillon once the liquid is absorbed.	4	Five minutes before the end of cooking, taste, and adjust the seasoning if necessary.	➤

5

Turn off the heat and add the cold butter and the Parmesan. Stir in rapidly then cover the pan and let rest for 2 minutes before serving.

HOMEMADE BOUILLON
❊

Bring to a boil 8 cups of water with 2 onions, 2 carrots, 2 celery stalks, and 2 leeks. Add salt and cook for 40 minutes then strain off the liquid. When you're pressed for time, use good-quality organic bouillon cubes. For meat stock, add to the vegetable base 1 lb of shin or stewing beef, a chicken or chicken thighs, and cook for 2 hours.

6	It's ready! Serve immediately because the risotto will continue to cook in its own heat.

VARIATION
❋

If any risotto is left over, shape into little cakes, dip into beaten egg then bread crumbs, and brown in a skillet.

WHICH VARIETY OF RISOTTO RICE?
❋

↞ Carnaroli is the easiest to cook without losing its shape.
↞ Arborio is the most widely available variety.
↞ Vialone nano is the rice of the Veneto, the region around Venice. It is ideal for very liquid risottos.

SAFFRON RISOTTO

❧ SERVES 4 • PREPARATION: 15 MINUTES • COOKING: 20 MINUTES ❧

Assemble the ingredients for a Classic Risotto (see recipe 50). Pour a ladleful of hot bouillon in a bowl, add 1 pinch of saffron threads, and let infuse.

Cook one beef marrow bone for 3 minutes in the bouillon, remove the bone, extract the marrow, and cut into pieces. Follow the steps for Classic Risotto, adding the marrow

pieces at the beginning with the onion, and soften everything for 10 minutes. Add the saffron and its liquid about three-quarters of the way into the cooking period.

MUSHROOM RISOTTO

❧ **SERVES 4** • PREPARATION: 30 MINUTES • COOKING: 30 MINUTES ❧

Clean 1¼ lb of fresh mushrooms. Heat 1 tablespoon of olive oil, 1 knob of butter, and 1 whole garlic clove in a skillet. Add the mushrooms and cook without stirring until they release all their liquid. Season with salt and pepper, lower the heat, and cook for a further 2–3 minutes. Discard the garlic, add ½ teaspoon chopped parsley, and keep warm. Follow the steps for Classic Risotto (see recipe 50), adding the mushrooms 5 minutes before the end of cooking.

SQUASH RISOTTO

❧ **SERVES 2** • PREPARATION: 20 MINUTES • COOKING: 30 MINUTES ❧

Heat 1 knob of butter in a skillet and cook 1 chopped shallot (or onion) until soft. Add ½ cup of puréed squash and season with 1 pinch of ground nutmeg, 1 pinch of powdered cinnamon, salt, and pepper. Follow the steps for Classic Risotto (see recipe 50), adding the chopped shallot instead of the onion. After 10 minutes, mix in the puréed squash and continue to add hot bouillon. Crush 1 amaretti cookie and sprinkle over the top to garnish the risotto before serving.

LEEK & COTECHINO RISOTTO

➤ **SERVES 2** • **PREPARATION: 20 MINUTES** • **COOKING: 30 MINUTES** ◄

Heat 1 tablespoon of olive oil and 1 knob of butter in a saucepan, then add 1 shallot and 2 chopped leeks (white parts only). Cook to soften then season with salt and pepper. Stir in the rice and follow the steps for Classic Risotto (see recipe 50). After 10 minutes, add 7 oz of cotechino, crumbled and continue to add hot chicken bouillon. (Note: if you cannot get hold of cotechino, use coarse-ground sausage meat, browned off in a skillet before adding it to the risotto.)

POTATO GNOCCHI

⇥ **SERVES 6** • PREPARATION: 30 MINUTES • COOKING: A FEW MINUTES ⇤

2 lb potatoes for mashing
1 cup plain flour
1 egg
salt, ground nutmeg

IN ADVANCE:
Wash the potatoes, cook for 40 minutes in
boiling salted water (or steam), then drain
and remove the skins.

1 2
3 4

1	Mash the peeled potatoes and let cool.	2	Make a well in the potato and pour in three-quarters of the flour, the egg, salt, and a pinch of nutmeg.	
3	Mix the ingredients, working from the center outward. Incorporate the remaining flour to give a smooth and even mixture.	4	Flour your hands and form the potato into long rolls about ¾ inch thick then cut them into mini log shapes about 1 inch in length.	➤

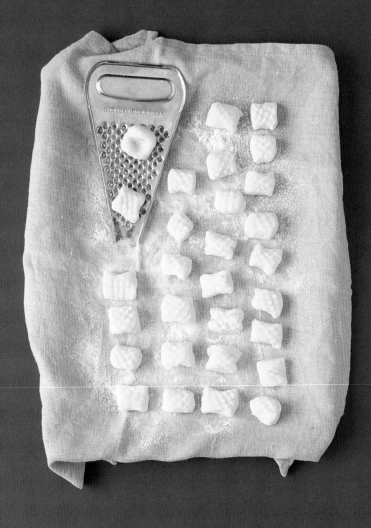

| 5 | Lightly press the gnocchi on the back of a shredder to form indentations (which help the sauce to cling) then place on a lightly floured kitchen towel. | **TIPS**
❊

☛ Don't prepare your gnocchi too long in advance (maximum 4 hours), otherwise they will become wet and sticky! If you have any left over, keep in a cool place in an oiled dish then quickly reheat in boiling water (do not keep them for longer than 24 hours). |

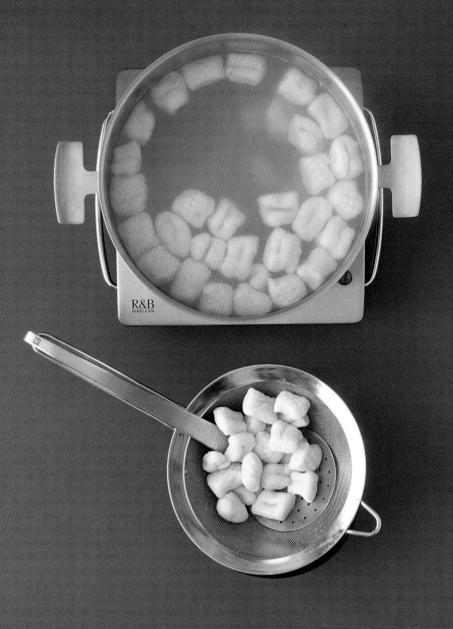

6

Bring a large pan of salted water to a boil. Add the gnocchi in two batches. They are cooked as soon as they rise up to the surface: remove them immediately with a slotted spoon.

FLAVORINGS
❀

↤ with 5–6 tablespoons sage or cinnamon-flavored butter and ⅔ cup shredded Parmesan.
↤ with Tomato Sauce (see recipe 40), and using a large pat of butter at the end in place of the oil.
↤ with Bolognaise Sauce (see recipe 36).
↤ with 5 oz Gorgonzola, melted with a little cream or milk.

ROMAN-STYLE GNOCCHI

⇢ **SERVES 6** • PREPARATION: 50 MINUTES • COOKING: 40 MINUTES ⇠

4 cups milk
1 cup fine semolina flour
10 tablespoons butter

salt
¾ cup freshly shredded Parmesan
2 egg yolks

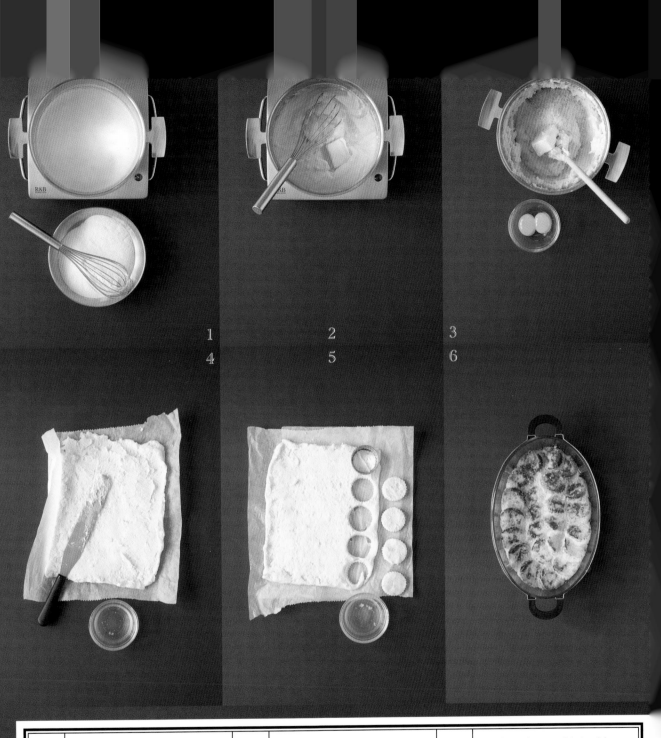

1	Bring the milk to a boil then tip in the semolina, stirring with a whisk.	2	Add 1½ tablespoons butter and the salt. Simmer for 20 minutes, stirring.	3	Off the heat, add 4 tablespoons butter and ½ cup Parmesan. Stir in the eggs.
4	Tip out the mixture onto a damp sheet of baking paper and spread it out evenly.	5	Use a wetted 2–2½-inch cookie cutter to press out rounds. Place in a greased ovenproof dish.	6	Top with the remaining Parmesan and butter, melted. Put in the oven for 15 minutes at 400°F.

FISH

4

CARPACCIO OF OCTOPUS

❖ **SERVES 8–12** • PREPARATION: 40 MINUTES • COOKING: 1 HOUR • CHILLING: 8 HOURS ❖

1 octopus weighing about 5 lb
POACHING BROTH:
2 celery stalks
2 onions and 2 carrots
½ bunch of parsley + 1 bay leaf
6 peppercorns, sea salt

TO SERVE:
juice of 1 lemon,
6 tablespoons olive oil
salt and pepper
8 oz arugula
3–4 celery stalks, cut into dice

1 cup black or green olives
½ bunch of parsley, chopped
IN ADVANCE:
Clean the octopus by emptying the head,
removing the eyes and beak, and thoroughly
rinsing the suckers.

1	Bring a large stockpot of water to the boil with all the poaching ingredients and a clean cork from a bottle (it helps to tenderize the octopus).	2	Holding it by the head, gently lower in the octopus. Cook for 50–60 minutes over a medium heat. Let cool in the cooking water.
3	Remove the octopus from the liquid and allow to rest a little (after cooking it will have shrunk by about two-thirds).	4	Cut off the top from a clean plastic bottle and pierce the base. Insert the octopus, packing it in firmly. Put in the fridge for 8 hours, weighted down. ➢

5	Cut the pressed octopus into thin slices.	**COOKING OCTOPUS** ❋ Octopus is cooked when you can easily insert a needle into one of the tentacles.
		DRESSING ❋ Mix the lemon juice with the olive oil, add some salt and pepper, and drizzle half of it over the arugula leaves.

6	Arrange the dressed arugula leaves over a large serving plate. Put the slices of octopus on top, then scatter with the diced celery and the olives. Drizzle with the remaining dressing and sprinkle with the chopped parsley.

STORING
❋

☞ Once cooked the octopus will freeze perfectly. Cover it well in plastic wrap.

SICILIAN-STYLE SWORDFISH

❧ **SERVES 2** • PREPARATION: 20 MINUTES • RESTING: 1 HOUR • COOKING: 15 MINUTES ❧

3 tablespoons salted capers
2 slices of swordfish (¾ in thick)
1 lemon
3 tablespoons olive oil, plus extra for cooking and greasing

2 anchovy fillets
1½ cups homemade bread crumbs
1 garlic clove
1 tablespoon oregano

IN ADVANCE:
Rinse then chop the capers (no need for more salt in this recipe). Preheat the oven to 350°F.

1 2
3 4

1	Put the swordfish in a nonmetallic dish and cover with the chopped capers, the grated peel of the lemon, and the olive oil. Let marinate for 1 hour.	2	Heat a little oil in a pan. Cook the anchovy fillets until they melt. Add the bread crumbs, garlic, cut in two (discard at the end), and oregano. Stir for 1 minute over a low heat.
3	Coat the fish with the bread-crumb mixture, transfer to an oiled baking dish, and drizzle over a little olive oil.	4	Transfer to the oven and cook for 15 minutes. Serve with ground pepper, a squeeze of lemon, and a tomato salad or Tomato Gratin (see recipe 25).

MARINATED BAKED SEA BREAM

❧ **SERVES 4 • PREPARATION: 15 MINUTES • MARINATING: 30 MINUTES • COOKING: 20 MINUTES** ❧

MARINADE:
1 small onion and 1 garlic clove
½ cup white wine
6 flat leaf parsley stalks
2 tablespoons olive oil

2 pinches sea salt
1 sea bream weighing about 2 lb (or sea bass
or scorpion fish), cleaned and scaled
½ cup mineral water + ½ oz sea salt
7 oz cherry tomatoes

IN ADVANCE:
Cut the onion for the marinade into rings
and the garlic into small pieces.

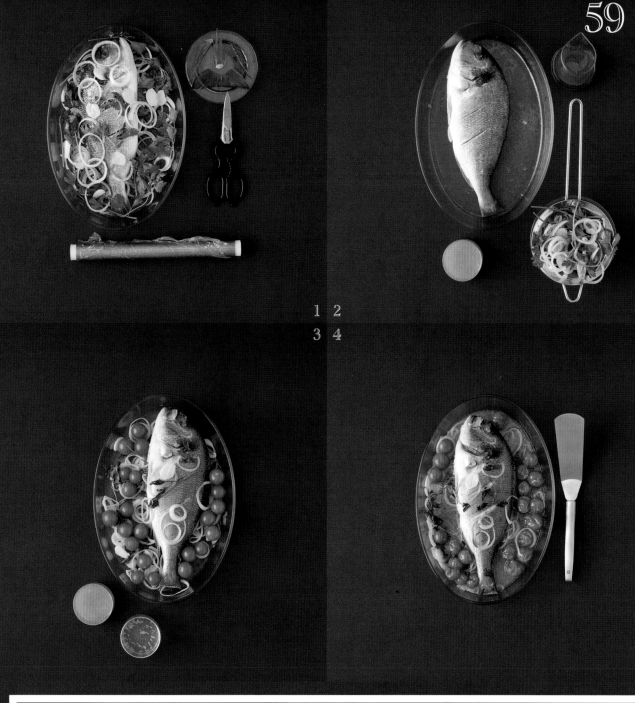

1	Make 2 cuts in both sides of the fish. Put in a nonmetallic ovenproof dish with the marinade ingredients, cover, and let stand for 30 minutes.	2	Remove everything, drain the fish, and return it to the dish. Brush with some of the oil then put in a preheated oven at 400°F.
3	Mix the marinade ingredients with the mineral water and sea salt. After the fish has baked for 5 minutes, pour in half the watered-down marinade along with the cherry tomatoes.	4	Cook for 8 minutes before pouring in the remainder of the watered-down marinade. Continue to cook for a further 5 minutes. Serve hot.

STUFFED SARDINES

❧ **SERVES 4** • PREPARATION: 30 MINUTES • COOKING: 15 MINUTES ❧

12 really fresh medium sardines
1½ cups homemade bread crumbs
4 anchovy fillets
1 heaping tablespoon salted capers
2 tablespoons raisins

3 tablespoons pine nuts
3 parsley stalks
2 mint stalks
juice of 1 small lemon and 1 orange
4 tablespoons olive oil

salt and freshly ground pepper
10–12 bay leaves
½ teaspoon sugar
1 tablespoon red wine vinegar

1 2
3 4

1	Clean and scale the sardines, then remove the heads and backbones. Rinse under running water, dry on paper towels, then open out flat down their length.	2	Whiz the bread crumbs in a mixer with the anchovies, capers, raisins, pine nuts, herbs, grated peel of the lemon, and 2–3 tablespoons olive oil. Taste before adding salt.
3	Spread 1 teaspoon of the mixture on the opened sardines, pressing it down, then roll them up toward the tail.	4	Pack the rolled sardines tightly into an ovenproof dish, tucking in a bay leaf between each one. ➤

5	Mix the orange and lemon juice with the sugar, vinegar, a drizzle of olive oil, and the pepper. Pour over the prepared sardines.	**TO SAVE TIME** ❀ You can ask your fishmonger to prepare the sardines.
		TIP ❀ The sardines must be really fresh. Do not buy ready filleted ones.

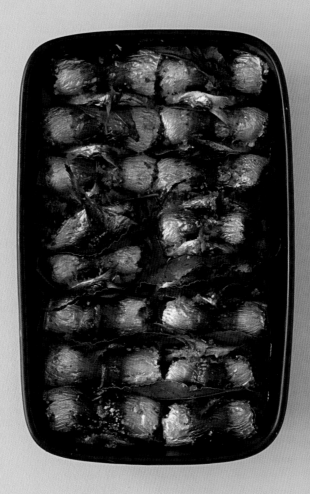

	Transfer to a preheated oven at 350°F for about 15 minutes. Serve warm or at room temperature with an arugula salad.	**WITH DRINKS** ✳
6		Once the sardines are cooked, cut each roll in half and spear with a toothpick.

BAKED SEA BASS WITH FEN

✣ SERVES 2 • PREPARATION: 15 MINUTES • COOKING: 15 MINUTES ✣

1 whole sea bass weighing about 1¼–1½ lb
2 fennel bulbs
olive oil
scant ½ cup fine semolina (pasta) flour or
cornstarch

salt and freshly ground pepper
½ teaspoon fennel seeds
1 tablespoon reduced balsamic vinegar
(see recipe 62)

IN ADVANCE:
Preheat the oven to 400

	TO CLEAN THE FISH	TO FILLET THE FISH
1	❧ Scale: Hold the fish by its tail and scrape off the scales using a firm-bladed knife. Rinse. ❧ Clean: Open up the belly and remove all the intestines. ❧ Trim: Cut off all fins and barbs, working from the head toward the tail.	❧ Bone: Dry the fish. Place on a chopping board with the cleaned belly toward you. Place a hand on top. Using a very sharp filleting knife, make an incision underneath and above the entire length of the dorsal spine, starting from the head. Slip the blade under the backbone and gently remove the fillet. Ease out the backbone and remove the second fillet.

2 3
4 5

2	Finely slice the fennel. Heat a little olive oil in a skillet and cook for 5 minutes (the slices should stay crisp). Season with salt and pepper.	3	Coat the fish fillets in the semolina flo shake them lightly to remove the exces
4	Heat 2 tablespoons of olive oil in a skillet. Cook the fillets, skin-side down, for 2 minutes. Season with salt.	5	Transfer the fillets to a baking tray line baking paper, top with lightly crushed seeds and cook in the oven for 4 minu

6 | Serve the bass on the fennel slices with the reduced balsamic vinegar drizzled on top.

TIPS
✳

☛ Try to buy line-caught bass for preference. You can always ask your fishmonger to clean and fillet the whole fish for you.

MEAT

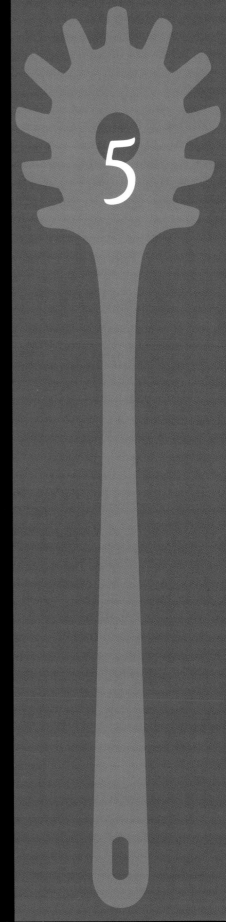

5

IN SLICES

PAN-FRIED

IN SAUCE

CARPACCIO OF BEEF

❧ **SERVES 6** • PREPARATION: 30 MINUTES ❧

6 tablespoons balsamic vinegar
1¼ lb best quality beef fillet (ask for the center cut)
olive oil

salt and freshly ground pepper
5 oz arugula leaves
3 oz Parmesan shavings
¾ cup black olives

IN ADVANCE:
Put the vinegar in a small saucepan over a medium heat and cook to reduce to a syrupy consistency.

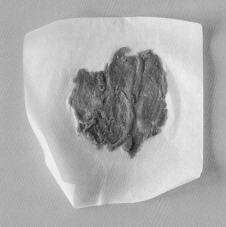

1 2
3 4

1	Cut the beef into very thin slices with a well-sharpened knife.	2	Cut out 12 squares of baking paper. Place 4–5 slices of beef side by side on half of the sheets.
3	Cover with the other 6 squares of paper then bat out the meat until very flat using a meat mallet.	4	Use kitchen scissors to cut the excess paper from around the meat so that they resemble dinner plates.

| 5 | Peel off the top sheet and invert the meat on a plate so that the second sheet of paper is uppermost. Peel that off too. Use a pastry brush to brush the beef slices with a little olive oil. | **TIP** ❋

☛ It's easier to cut the meat into very thin slices if you put the piece in the freezer, covered tightly in plastic wrap, before cutting it. |

6   At the point of serving, season the beef with salt and pepper. Top with some arugula leaves dressed with 2 tablespoons of olive oil, some salt, and some pepper. Garnish with Parmesan shavings, black olives, and a drizzle of reduced balsamic vinegar.

IN ADVANCE
❀

You can make the carpaccio ahead of serving if you cover it well with plastic wrap and keep in the fridge.

CARPACCIO EXPRESS
❀

☛ Ask your butcher to prepare the thin slices on a bacon slicer, or buy beef ready-sliced for carpaccio.

VEAL IN TUNA SAUCE

⇸ **SERVES 6–8** • PREPARATION: 20 MINUTES • COOKING: 40 MINUTES ⇷

1 onion
1 carrot
1 celery stalk
several flat leaf parsley stalks
2 lb boneless veal topside

TUNA SAUCE:
10 oz tuna in oil, drained
6 anchovy fillets
1½ tablespoons capers (preferably salted)
1 handful of flat leaf parsley

½ cup mayonnaise
salt and freshly ground pepper
IN ADVANCE:
Peel and chop all the vegetables and finely chop the parsley.

1 2
3 4

1	Put the vegetables into a large pan of salted water and bring to a boil. Add the veal, return to a boil, and cook for 25 minutes. Let cool in the stock.	2	For the sauce, blend the tuna, anchovies, half the capers and parsley, mayonnaise, and ¾ cup of cold bouillon. Season then keep cool.
3	Cut the veal into very thin slices (you could also ask your butcher to do this in advance).	4	Arrange the veal on a dish, cover with sauce, and sprinkle with remaining capers and parsley. Serve with arugula and Tomato Gratin (see recipe 25).

FILLET OF BEEF

❧ **SERVES 2** • PREPARATION: 10 MINUTES • MARINADE: 1 HOUR • COOKING: 5 MINUTES ❧

balsamic vinegar
10 oz beef fillet (¾-inch thick slice)
olive oil
3 rosemary stalks

salt flakes and freshly ground pepper
3½ oz arugula leaves
¾ oz Parmesan shavings

IN ADVANCE:
Reduce 4 tablespoons of balsamic vinegar
(see recipe 62).

1 2
3 4

1	Brush the beef with olive oil and sprinkle with rosemary. Place in a dish, cover with plastic wrap, and let marinate for 1 hour at room temperature.	2	Preheat a ridged griddle pan and cook the meat for 2 minutes on each side (longer if you like it more cooked). Generously season with salt and pepper and keep warm.
3	Pour 1 or 2 tablespoons water into the pan, scraping up the bits stuck to the base, and allow the juices to reduce.	4	Cut the meat into 8 pieces. Serve with the arugula leaves dressed with the meat juices and the balsamic vinegar, and the Parmesan.

MILAN-STYLE VEAL ESCALOPES

❧ **SERVES 2 • PREPARATION: 20 MINUTES • COOKING: 5 MINUTES** ❧

2 veal escalopes
4 or 5 slices of fresh bread (soft batch,
crusts removed), made into crumbs
1 egg

1 tablespoon butter
2 tablespoons olive oil
1 lemon
salt

IN ADVANCE:
Use a meat mallet to flatten the veal to
⅛ inch thick between 2 sheets of baking
paper. Reduce the bread to crumbs in a mixer.

1 2
3 4

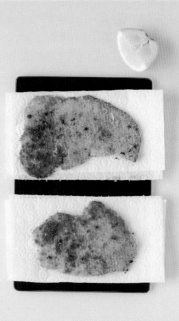

1	Beat the egg in a shallow dish and spread the bread crumbs on a sheet of baking paper.	2	Dip both sides of the escalopes first in egg then in bread crumbs, pressing them in firmly to make sure they stick.
3	Melt the butter with the oil in a skillet and fry the escalopes on both sides until golden-brown.	4	Dry the escalopes on paper towel, season with salt, and serve hot or cold with a wedge of lemon and tomato salad.

SALTIMBOCCA

❖ **SERVES 2** • PREPARATION: 15 MINUTES • COOKING: 8 MINUTES ❖

2 veal escalopes weighing about
5 oz each
2 thin slices of Parma ham
4 sage leaves

1 tablespoon olive oil
2 tablespoons butter
2 cups dry white wine or water
pinch of salt

TIP:
If you don't have a meat mallet, you can bat
out the meat with the base of a small heavy
saucepan.

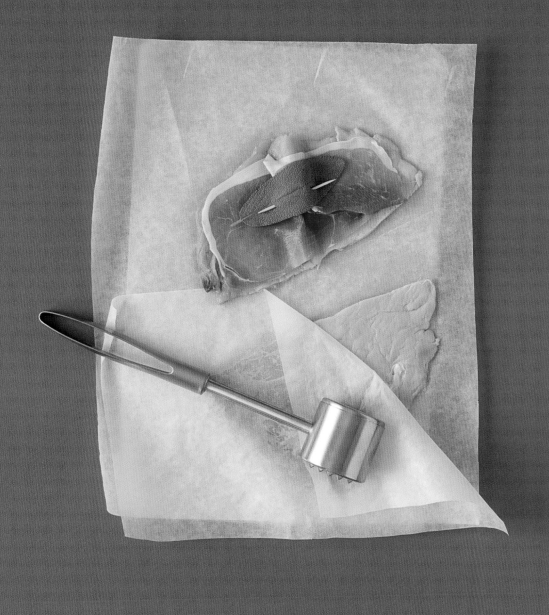

1 Place the escalopes between 2 sheets of baking parchment and use a meat mallet to gently bat them out very thinly. Place ½ slice of ham and 1 sage leaf on each escalope and secure with a toothpick.

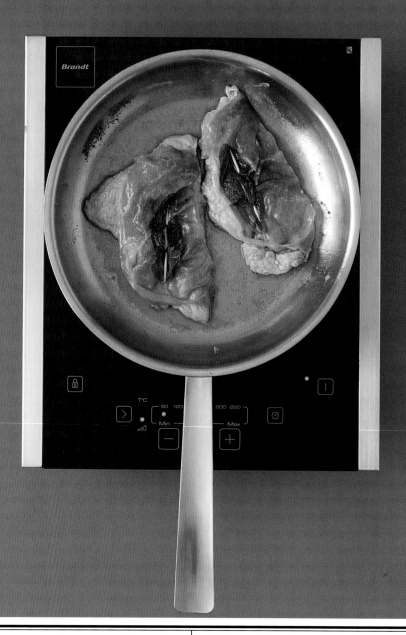

| 2 | Heat the oil and two-thirds of the butter in a skillet over a medium-high heat. Cook the escalopes, first on the ham side then on the other side (about 5 minutes in total). Remove and keep warm while you make the sauce. | **TO MAKE THE SAUCE**
❋

☛ Pour the wine or water into the skillet, scraping up the caramelized bits on the base. Let boil for 1 minute then add the remaining butter and a pinch of salt. |

3 Pour the sauce over the escalopes and serve
with a salad of arugula leaves or with seasonal
vegetables.

CHICKEN & RICOTTA PARCEL

❧ **SERVES 6** • PREPARATION: 20 MINUTES • COOKING: 40 MINUTES ❧

1 lb chicken breasts
2 cups ricotta
½ cup freshly shredded Parmesan
2 egg yolks
salt and freshly ground pepper
3 pinches of ground nutmeg

10–12 slices Parma ham or speck (smoked cured ham)
knob of butter
1 tablespoon olive oil
sage leaves
3 tablespoons dry white wine

IN ADVANCE:
Remove any fat from the chicken and finely chop (easiest in a food-mixer). Preheat the oven to 350°F.

1 2
3 4

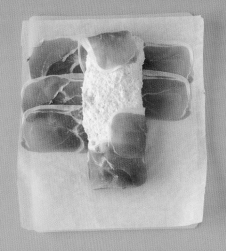

1	Mix the chicken meat with the ricotta, the shredded Parmesan, the egg yolks, salt, pepper, and nutmeg.	2	Turn out the mixture onto the center of a sheet of baking paper and form into a thick log.
3	On another piece of paper, arrange the Parma ham slices, slightly overlapping. Put the shaped mixture in the center and wrap with the slices.	4	Cover the chicken mixture completely with the ham slices. ➤

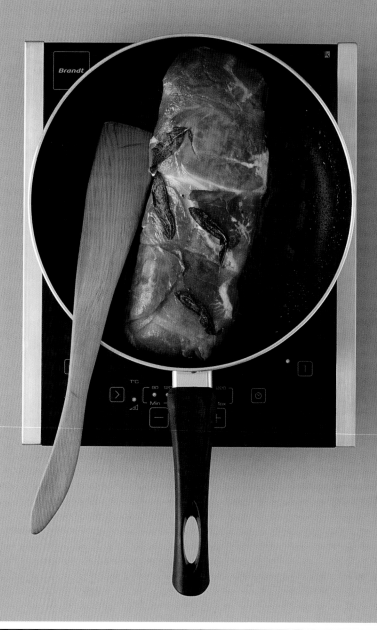

| 5 | Heat the butter and the oil in a large skillet with the sage leaves. Place the wrapped parcel in the pan and brown on all sides. | **ALTERNATIVE**
❈

☛ You can completely cook the parcel in the skillet, covered with a lid or aluminum foil, over a low heat. |

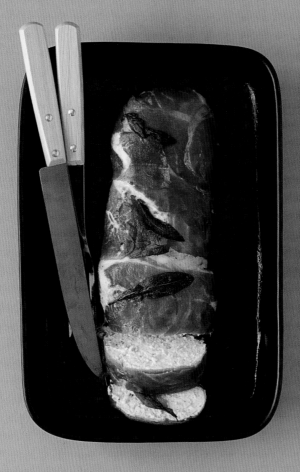

		VARIATION
6	Transfer the parcel to a baking tray and continue to cook in the oven for 30 minutes. After 10 minutes, pour in the white wine, allow it to evaporate, then cover the tray with aluminum foil. Serve cut into slices, with vegetables.	Use ground veal instead of chicken.

GUINEAFOWL IN PEPPER SAUCE

SERVES 4 • PREPARATION: 30 MINUTES • COOKING: 1 HOUR

1 guineafowl weighing at least 2 lb
3½ oz lardo di Colonnata (cured pork fat)
or pancetta, sliced finely
2 rosemary stalks
1 tablespoon butter + 2 tablespoons olive oil
2 bay leaves + 4 garlic cloves, chopped small

salt and freshly ground pepper
5 fl oz dry white wine
PEPPER SAUCE:
7 oz chicken livers
giblets from the guineafowl
3½ oz sopressa (a cured sausage)

1 lemon
2 garlic cloves
5 fl oz olive oil
5 fl oz dry white wine
salt and freshly ground pepper
1 bunch of flat leaf parsley, chopped

1 2
3 4

1	Put the untrussed guineafowl on a board, stretch over slices of the pork fat, and stuff the remainder into the cavity with the rosemary.	2	Truss the bird with kitchen string.	
3	Heat the butter and oil in a large pan, add the bay leaves and garlic, and brown the guineafowl on all sides. Season with salt and pepper. Drain and discard the fat from the pan.	4	Transfer the bird to the oven at 400°F for 40 minutes. After 10 minutes, pour over the wine, then, at regular intervals, a little water.	➢

5 6
7 8

5	To make the sauce, trim the chicken livers and giblets and chop the sopressa. Zest the lemon and squeeze the juice.	6	Put all these ingredients, except the lemon juice, in a food-mixer with 1 garlic clove. Finely chop.
7	Heat the olive oil in a saucepan with the second garlic clove (discarding it as soon as the oil is hot). Add the chicken liver mixture and brown, stirring.	8	Add the wine and juices from the guineafowl. Add a little salt and plenty of pepper. Cook gently for 10 minutes, add the lemon juice and parsley and cook for a further 5 minutes.

9

To serve, cut the guineafowl into 4, coat with the pepper sauce and accompany with polenta (see recipe 72).

 Instead of the sopressa you can use 8 anchovy fillets. For a slightly more tart-tasting sauce, use 4–5 tablespoons of vinegar in place of lemon juice.

MILAN-STYLE OSSO BUCO

❧ **SERVES 4** • PREPARATION: 30 MINUTES • COOKING: 1 HOUR 30 MINUTES ❧

2 onions
4 slices of shin of veal, about 2 inches thick
⅓ cup all-purpose flour
4 tablespoons olive oil

5 tablespoons butter
⅔ cup dry white wine
salt and freshly ground pepper
1–1¼ cups meat bouillon

GREMOLATA:
1 garlic clove
1 bunch of flat leaf parsley, 1 untreated lemon
IN ADVANCE:
Chop the onions very finely.

1 2
3 4

1	Make 3 small cuts around the sides of the shin slices so that they remain flat during cooking, then lightly dust with flour.	2	Heat half the oil and a third of the butter in a Dutch oven. Add the onions and cook very gently for 20 minutes. Remove and set aside.
3	Add the remaining oil and another third of the butter to the pan. Brown the veal slices for 5 minutes on each side. Return the onions.	4	Pour in the white wine, leave to evaporate for 6–7 minutes, season with salt and pepper, and add ½ cup bouillon.

➢

5 6
7 8

5	Cover the pot and cook over a very low heat for 1 hour 20 minutes (or in the oven in a shallow dish, covered with a sheet of buttered aluminum foil, at 350°F).	6	As it cooks, turn the meat from time to time and keep topping up with a little of the remaining bouillon as the sauce thickens.
7	To make the gremolata, crush the garlic then finely chop the flat leaf parsley with the garlic and the peel of half the lemon.	8	The meat is cooked when it falls off the bones. Remove the pieces and blend the sauce with the remaining butter and half the gremolata.

| 9 | Replace the meat in the casserole and reheat gently for 2 minutes. Serve sprinkled with the remaining gremolata, accompanied with Saffron Risotto (see recipe 51). | **VARIATION**
❋
Add ¾ cup of peeled, deseeded, and chopped tomatoes before covering the casserole in step 5.

TIP
❋
☛ For the most succulent flavor, buy milk-fed veal. |

VEAL STEW WITH POLENTA

❧ **SERVES 6** • PREPARATION: 30 MINUTES • COOKING: 1 HOUR 30 MINUTES ❧

3 lb stewing veal
2 onions
2 carrots
2 celery stalks
1 garlic clove

1½ tablespoons butter
4 tablespoons olive oil
6 sage leaves
1 rosemary stalk
½ cup dry white wine

1 lb 12 oz canned chopped tomatoes
meat bouillon (optional)
salt and freshly ground pepper
Polenta made with 1 lb cornmeal (see recipe 72)

1 2
3 4

1	Cut the meat into 2-inch cubes and finely chop all the vegetables.	2	Heat the butter and oil in a Dutch oven and seal the meat pieces in 2 batches, for 5 minutes each batch. Remove and keep warm.
3	Add the vegetables to the pot and cook for a few minutes.	4	Return the meat with the herbs, allow to brown, then pour in the wine and stir until it evaporates. ➤

5

Reduce the sauce before adding the chopped tomatoes. Cover the pot and leave to gently simmer over a very low heat for 1 hour. If the sauce reduces too much, add a little extra bouillon or water.

VARIATION
❋

For a white veal stew, use all bouillon instead of adding tomatoes. You can also equally use cubed beef, lamb, or chine of pork in this recipe and add spices or other herbs.

		TO SERVE
		❋
6	Season with salt and pepper at the end of cooking and serve with hot polenta.	Accompany with a selection of seasonal vegetables.

POLENTA

❖ COOKING: 5 MINUTES FOR PRECOOKED POLENTA, 45 MINUTES FOR CORNMEAL ❖

salt
1 lb yellow cornmeal for polenta (either
precooked or uncooked)

8¾ cups water (use 10 cups for wetter polenta
or 6¼ cups for a firm polenta)

QUANTITIES:
Allow 4–5 times the amount of water to
polenta.

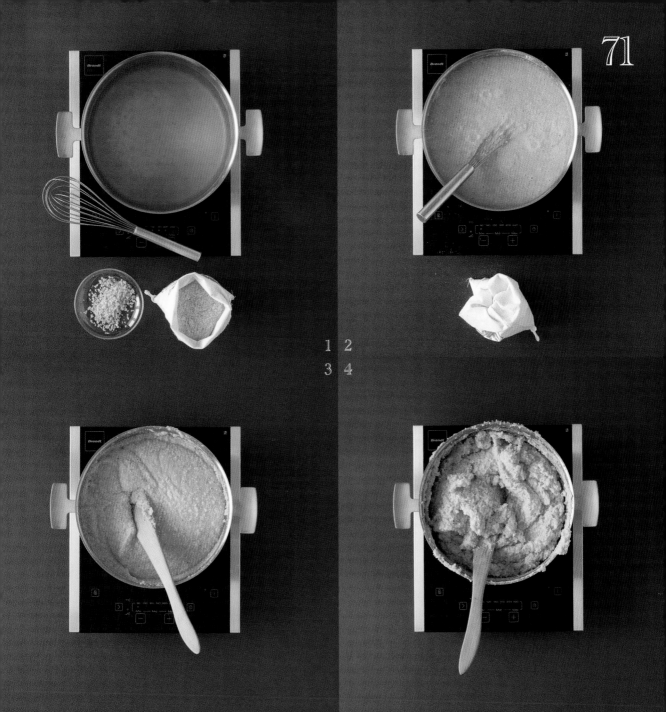

1	Bring a large pot of water (see quantities) to a boil and add ½ oz salt for every 4 cups of water.	2	Once the water is boiling, pour in the cornmeal in a steady stream, whisking constantly to avoid any lumps.	
3	Reduce the heat until the mix only slightly bubbles. Continue to cook for about 5 minutes if using precooked polenta or for 45 minutes for cornmeal, stirring with a wooden spoon.	4	Add extra water for a wetter polenta. It is cooked when it starts to come away from the sides of the pan.	➤

	TO SERVE ❈	**VARIATION** ❈
5	Put the hot polenta on a wooden board to serve, or press into a dampened mold to present in a shape. A wetter polenta is served with a spoon. Polenta can be served with meat or fish in a sauce, with cheese, cooked meats, pan-fried mushrooms, and so forth.	For a richer polenta, use half water and half milk. You can add a knob of butter or shredded Parmesan.
		SUGGESTION ❈
		Just before the end of cooking, add some cooked mushrooms, chopped olives, or sun-dried tomatoes.

6 7
8 9

POLENTA GRATIN	POLENTA WITH GORGONZOLA
6 Allow the polenta to cool, cut into pieces, and reheat in the oven or in a skillet with a little butter.	7 Top the hot polenta with Gorgonzola or other strongly flavored cheese.
POLENTA WITH SAUSAGES	POLENTA WITH MUSHROOMS
8 Serve the polenta with fried sausages or with sopressa (a soft cured sausage).	9 Serve with pan-fried mixed wild mushrooms (see recipe 34).

DESSERTS

6

CREAMY

CAKES & TARTS

TIRAMISU

❖ **SERVES 4** • PREPARATION: 30 MINUTES • CHILLING: 2 HOURS MINIMUM ❖

3 small, really fresh eggs
3 tablespoons white sugar
3 tablespoons dry marsala

1 cup chilled mascarpone
3½ oz Pavesini biscuits or
sponge fingers (ladyfingers)

4 shots hot espresso
1 tablespoon unsweetened cocoa powder
1 pinch of salt

1 2
3 4

1	Separate the eggs.	2	Use a hand-held electric beater to beat the egg yolks with the sugar until light and creamy.	
3	Add the marsala and mascarpone to the egg mixture, a little at a time.	4	Beat for a few more minutes until you have a smooth, thick cream. Put in the fridge to keep cold.	➤

5 6
7 8

5	Whip the egg whites with the salt into firm peaks.	6	Use a whisk to gently incorporate the beaten egg whites into the mascarpone mixture.
7	Spread 2 tablespoons of the mixture in the base of a shallow-sided square or oblong dish. Quickly soak the biscuits in the hot coffee and arrange a layer on top of the cream mixture.	8	Cover the biscuits with more cream and build up 2 further layers in this way, finishing with a layer of cream. Chill in the fridge for a minimum of 2 hours.

9	To serve, dust the top with the unsweetened cocoa powder sifted through a tea strainer.	**TIP** ❈ ☛ Eat tiramisu within 24 hours because it contains raw eggs.
VARIATION ❈		**SUMMER TIRAMISU** ❈
You can make the dessert with slices of sponge cake that has gone a little dry (build up 2 layers only).		Instead of coffee, use strawberry coulis (see recipe 73), thinned with a little orange juice, and decorate with red berries before serving.

PANNA COTTA

❧ **SERVES 8** • PREPARATION: 15 MINUTES • COOKING: 10 MINUTES • CHILLING: ABOUT 3 HOURS ❧

4 cups heavy or whipping cream
1 vanilla bean, split in two

grated peel of 1 untreated lemon
3 tablespoons vanilla-flavored powder for
making crème caramel (sold in sachets)

TIP:
If you can't find the vanilla powder, use
3 tablespoons sugar + 1 sachet (½ oz)
powdered gelatin or 1 teaspoon agar-agar.

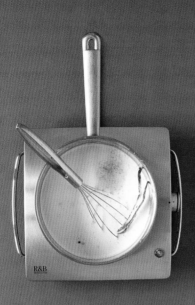

1 2
3 4

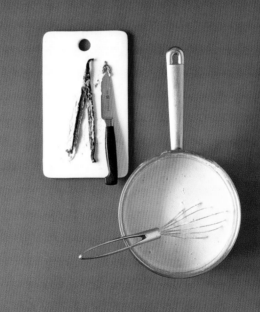

1	Put the cream with the vanilla bean, and the lemon peel in a pan and gently heat, stirring, for 3 minutes.	2	Sprinkle in the vanilla powder, stirring constantly.	
3	Continue to stir with the whisk until the cream starts to bubble.	4	Remove from the heat, remove the vanilla bean and scrape any remaining seeds into the cream. Let cool for 5 minutes, stirring from time to time.	➤

		VARIATION
5	Rinse 8 molds or ramekin dishes with water but don't dry them; this will make it easier to slip out the desserts. Pour the cream mixture into a jug then fill the molds. Let cool completely before covering with plastic wrap and chilling in the fridge for 3 hours.	You can flavor your panna cotta with a little marsala or rum, with flower waters (rose- or orange-flower), with fruit syrup, infusions, or spices. For a coffee-flavored version, add 3 tablespoons sugar and 3 teaspoons instant powdered coffee.

6

To turn out the desserts, run the point of a knife round the rims, put a plate on top, and quickly invert, giving each one a sharp shake.

TO SERVE
— ❊ —

For a fresh coulis of strawberries (or other red fruits), blend 1 lb strawberries with 3 tablespoons sugar and a squeeze of lemon juice. Rub everything through a fine-mesh sieve, adding a little water if necessary to give a pouring consistency. Otherwise, try serving with a drizzle of caramel or a reduction of balsamic vinegar (see recipe 62).

SABAYON

➤ SERVES 6 • PREPARATION: 15 MINUTES • COOKING: 10 MINUTES ◄

6 egg yolks
½ cup granulated raw cane sugar
½ cup dry marsala

ALTERNATIVE:
Mix the chilled sabayon with 1 cup of
whipped cream and serve with fresh fruits.

1 2
3 4

1	Mix the egg yolks, sugar, and marsala in a bowl and set over a pan of barely simmering hot water.	2	Beat everything together using a hand-held electric beater.
3	After about 5 minutes you should have a thick mousse-like mixture.	4	Serve the sabayon hot or warm with biscuits. To chill it (see alternative), plunge the bowl in ice water and stir frequently.

SEMIFREDDO

❖ **SERVES 10** • PREPARATION: 30 MINUTES • FREEZING: 6 HOURS ❖

7 oz almond torrone (nougat)
3½ oz dark chocolate (70% cocoa solids)
2 cups chilled heavy or whipping cream
1 Sabayon (see recipe 74), cooled

IN ADVANCE:
Oil a large loaf pan (or 10 individual molds)
and line with plastic wrap.

RED FRUIT VERSION:
Mix 14 oz cleaned red berries and 1 cup
whipped cream with the cooled sabayon.

1 2
3 4

1	Roughly chop the torrone and chocolate.	2	Whip the cream and fold into the cooled sabayon.
3	Spread one-third of the nougat and chocolate in the lined pan and cover with one-third of the cream. Repeat twice. Freeze for 6 hours.	4	Remove the semifreddo from the freezer about 10 minutes before serving. Quickly dip the pan into hot water and turn out the semifreddo.

CHOCOLATE AMARETTI CAKE

❧ SERVES 6–8 • PREPARATION: 30 MINUTES • COOKING: 25 MINUTES ❧

3½ oz dark chocolate (70% cocoa solids)
7 tablespoons butter + an extra knob
3 oz amaretti de Sorreno
3 eggs
⅔ cup superfine sugar

scant ½ cup all-purpose flour
¼ teaspoon baking soda
½ cup toasted almonds

GANACHE:
3½ oz dark chocolate
½ cup light or whipping cream
IN ADVANCE:
Preheat the oven to 350°F.

1 2
3 4

1	Break up the chocolate and put in a bowl with the butter, cut into pieces. Set the bowl over a pan of barely simmering hot water.	2	Whiz the amaretti in a food-mixer or crush to crumbs with a rolling pin.
3	Generously grease an 8-inch round cake pan with the knob of butter. Use the amaretti crumbs to line the base and the sides. Chill in the fridge.	4	Beat the eggs and sugar until they are light and creamy. ➤

5 6
7 8

5	Sift in the flour with the baking soda, incorporate with the whisk, then add in the cooled melted chocolate.	6	Pour into the pan and transfer to the oven for 25 minutes. Insert the point of a knife into the middle of the cake: it should come out clean.
7	To make the ganache, melt the chocolate and cream in a bowl set over a saucepan of barely simmering hot water.	8	Let the cake cool for 5 minutes before turning out on a wire rack. Spread the ganache over the surface using a plastic spatula.

		TIP
9	Decorate the cake with the toasted almonds, roughly chopped.	☞ You can bake the cake the day before and make the ganache topping the following day.

SWEET SHORT PIE PASTRY

❧ **ENOUGH FOR A TART TO SERVE 8** • PREPARATION: 10 MINUTES • RESTING: 1 HOUR ❧

2 cups all-purpose flour
8 tablespoons butter at room temperature, cubed
2 egg yolks

⅓ cup superfine sugar
1 pinch of salt
grated peel of 1 untreated lemon
2 tablespoons marsala (or water)

PASTRY IN THE FOOD-MIXER:
Put the flour and cold butter into the bowl and whiz for 10 seconds. Add the remaining ingredients and whiz again for 30 seconds. Form into a ball.

1 2
3 4

1	Sift the flour onto a pastry board and use your fingertips to rub in the butter to form bread crumbs.	2	Make a well in the center and drop in the egg yolks, sugar, salt, lemon peel, and marsala.
3	Mix everything together with your fingertips, bringing together all the crumbs without overworking the dough.	4	Form into a ball then flatten to a thickness of about a good inch. Wrap in plastic wrap and place in the fridge to rest for 1 hour.

RICOTTA, PINE NUT, & RAISIN TART

➻ **SERVES 8** • PREPARATION: 30 MINUTES • COOKING: 1 HOUR ❧

3 tablespoons raisins
1 Sweet Short Pie Pastry (see recipe 77)
2 cups ricotta
4 tablespoons pine nuts
2 eggs

3 tablespoons melted butter
⅔ cup superfine sugar
½ level teaspoon powdered cinnamon
grated peel of 1 untreated lemon
4 tablespoons marsala

IN ADVANCE:
Soak the raisins for 10 minutes in a bowl of warm water. Drain, then sprinkle them with a little flour.

1 2
3 4

1	Work the rested dough for 30 seconds then roll out on a lightly floured pastry board.	2	Butter and flour a tart pan then line with the pastry. Prick the base with a fork and return to the fridge to rest.
3	Mix the ricotta until smooth then add all the remaining ingredients, including the soaked raisins. Stir to combine.	4	Pour the mixture into the lined pan. Use your fingers to press down the sides of the pastry to meet the level of the filling. ➢

5	Cook in a preheated oven at 325°F for 1 hour. If the surface is becoming brown too quickly, cover with aluminum foil.	**VARIATIONS** ❀
		Flavor the tart with the finely grated rind of 1 untreated orange and make the pastry with orange water instead of marsala. You can add to the filling a little preserved ginger or candied lemon and orange peel.

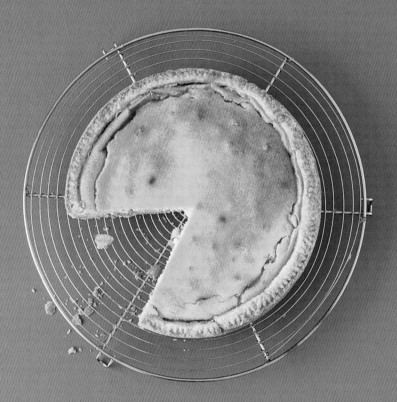

| 6 | Remove the tart from the oven and cool on a wire rack before cutting into portions. | **TIP** ❋ — ☞ You can make the pastry the day before and serve the tart over the next 2 days. Keep it cool. |

RED FRUIT TARTLETS

➤ **MAKES 25–30 TARTLETS** • PREPARATION: 20 MINUTES • COOKING: 15 MINUTES ➤

1 Sweet Short Pie Pastry (see recipe 77)
generous ½ cup mascarpone
1 cup ricotta
⅜ cup confectioners' sugar

1 sachet vanilla sugar
grated peel of 1 lemon
2 tablespoons sweet wine (muscat)
½ punnet raspberries

½ punnet strawberries
2 handfuls of cherries, pitted
IN ADVANCE:
Preheat the oven to 350°F.

1	Thinly roll out the pastry on a lightly floured pastry board. Use a floured 4-inch cookie cutter to cut out 25–30 disks.	2	Transfer the pastry disks to a baking sheet covered in baking paper. Prick the pastry with a fork.	
3	Cook in the preheated oven until the pastry is golden (about 15 minutes). Transfer to a wire rack and let cool.	4	Put the mascarpone and the ricotta in a bowl with the sugars, lemon rind, and sweet wine. Work smooth with a spoon.	➤

5	Spread a small teaspoonful of the cream mixture on each pastry disk then top with a whole raspberry, pieces of strawberry, and the pitted cherries.	**TIP** ❋ You can make and bake the pastry disks in advance and decorate them with the cream and the fruits just before you are ready to serve.

	It's ready!	**VARIATION** ❋
6		This pastry is enough to make 1 large tart (8–9 inch diameter). For the filling you would need to use 1 cup mascarpone, 1 cup ricotta, and ½ cup confectioners' sugar.

AUNTIE'S RICE CAKE

❧ **SERVES 8–10** • PREPARATION: 20 MINUTES • COOKING: 55 MINUTES ❧

4 cups whole milk
1 pinch of salt
¾ cup risotto rice (carnaroli or arborio)
1⅓ cups superfine sugar

1 tablespoon grated peel of 1 untreated lemon
6 tablespoons marsala
3 eggs + 1 tablespoon confectioners' sugar

IN ADVANCE:
Preheat the oven to 350°F. Butter and flour a large ovenproof dish or baking pan.

1	Put the milk and the salt in a large pan and bring to a boil.	2	Tip in the rice and stir with a wooden spoon. Cook over a gentle heat for 8 minutes (the rice should remain al dente).	
3	Let cool, stirring from time to time (if you transfer it to a bowl, it will cool faster).	4	Once the rice has cooled, add the superfine sugar, the lemon rind, and 4 tablespoons of the marsala.	➤

5 6
7 8

5	Separate the eggs and add the yolks to the rice, one at a time, incorporating with a whisk.	6	Lightly beat the egg whites with a fork and incorporate into the rice mixture.
7	Drain the rice through a colander over a bowl, reserving the liquid.	8	Fill the prepared dish or pan with the drained rice, then pour the reserved liquid on top: this way the rice settles in the bottom of the dish and a light crust forms on the surface. Transfer the dish to the oven and bake for 45 minutes.

9   When cooked, remove from the oven and sprinkle with the confectioners' sugar and the remaining 2 tablespoons of marsala. Serve the rice warm or at room temperature, either cut into squares or large spoonfuls.

VARIATION
❈

☛ Instead of flouring the dish, you can sprinkle it with a coating of crushed amaretti over the base, rather than flour.

TIP
❈

☛ The rice cake tastes even better if it can rest for 2 hours after it comes out of the oven.

BAKED PEACHES

➤ **SERVES 4** • PREPARATION: 20 MINUTES • COOKING: 30 MINUTES ⬅

4 perfectly ripe yellow peaches
6 oz amaretti di Sassello (8–10 biscuits)
1 egg yolk
1 tablespoon unsweetened cocoa powder

1 tablespoon butter
1 small glass of sweet wine (muscat)
½ teaspoon confectioners' sugar (optional)

IN ADVANCE:
Preheat the oven to 350°F.
Note: You can prepare this dessert the day
before, and cook it when you want to serve.

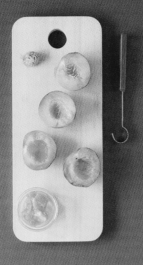

1 2
3 4

1	Cut the peaches in half (do not peel them), remove the stone, then hollow out the center slightly, reserving the flesh.	2	Blend the amaretti with the egg yolk, cocoa powder, and reserved peach flesh.
3	Stuff the peach halves with the amaretti mixture. Place in a buttered gratin dish, and dot the remaining butter on the peaches. Pour over the sweet wine.	4	Cook the peaches in the preheated oven for 20 minutes. Baste them with the juices once or twice as they cook. Serve warm or at room temperature.

RICH PANDORO DESSERT

❖ MAKES 14 SLICES • PREPARATION: 30 MINUTES ❖

1 pandoro (Italian sweet yeast bread)
MASCARPONE CREAM:
1 cup mascarpone + 3 egg yolks
3 tablespoons granulated sugar
4 tablespoons marsala, amaretto, or rum)

1 cup chilled heavy cream
2 punnets of red berries (red currants, black currants, raspberries)
handful of red candies
1 tablespoon confectioners' sugar

☛ If you want to slice the pandoro in advance, put it back in its wrapping so that it doesn't dry out, and then layer it at the last moment. You can use other spirits, such as whiskey, for this dessert, too.

1 2
3 4

1	Work the mascarpone until smooth. Beat the egg yolks with the sugar and alcohol until they are light and creamy.	2	Add the mascarpone to the egg mixture and continue to beat until you have a smooth and thick cream.	
3	Whip the cream. Gently incoporate it into the mascarpone mixture with the whisk.	4	Cut the pandoro across its width to give slices about 1 inch thick. Cut the very largest slices in half or in thirds.	➤

5	Now reassemble the pandoro on a serving plate but alternating the slices with a layer of the mascarpone cream (spread it with a spatula or pipe it on if you prefer), and fruit scattered on each layer.

A NOTE ON PANDORO
❋

Pandoro, along with panettone, is found throughout Italy at Christmas time. It is a sweet yeast bread, rather like brioche but star-shaped, which originated in Verona. It takes so long to prepare that all Italians buy their pandoro, provided they can find a good-quality one! Traditionally pandoro is served just as it is, with a simple dusting of confectioners' sugar.

6	Decorate with more fruit and scatter around the red candies. Lightly dust the surface with confectioners' sugar (this is provided with the pandoro), sifting it through a tea strainer.	**TO SERVE** ❄ Cut in slices and serve using a cake slicer.

APPENDICES

GLOSSARY

MENUS

TABLE OF CONTENTS

RECIPE INDEX

GENERAL INDEX

ACKNOWLEDGMENTS

GLOSSARY

AMARETTI
Little cookies made from bitter almonds. Amaretti di Sassello are soft; Amaretti di Saronno are crunchy.

ANCHOVIES
For preference, select the salted version when anchovies are to be cooked in a recipe and anchovies preserved in olive oil for all other dishes.

BALSAMIC VINEGAR
Look for the one from Reggio Emilia or Modena, with no additives or coloring (or a maximum of 2% caramel). See also Reduction of Balsamic Vinegar.

BARD, BARDING
This refers to stretching slices of bacon, or cured or fatty ham, over meat or poultry to prevent it drying out during cooking.

BASIL
The quintessential Italian herb, and a staple ingredient in tomato sauces for pasta and, of course, in classic pesto.

BLACK OLIVES
When possible, look for the Italian variety called taggiasca (pronounced tadgiaska). Similar varieties are those from Gaeta or Lucca, otherwise you can use the small black French olives produced around Nice.

BORLOTTI
A pinkish-brown bean that is essential for a good bean soup. They are usually sold dried and in tins but in season you can find fresh borlotti in their pods.

BOTARGO (OR POUTARGUE)
This luxury ingredient is made from the dried eggs of gray mullet, preserved with either beeswax or paraffin wax. It is shredded or shaved over a dish. Botargo made from tuna eggs has a stronger taste and a more pronounced iodine flavor.

BOUILLON
If you don't have time to make your own vegetable- or meat-based bouillon, make sure you buy good-quality bouillon cubes, preferably organic.

BREAD CRUMBS
These recipes use homemade bread crumbs, made from stale bread reduced to crumbs in a food-mixer.

BRESAOLA
This is air-dried, salt-cured beef. It is sold thinly sliced; look for it in good supermarkets and delicatessens.

BURRATA
A fresh cheese made from mozzarella and cream. It is very delicate and should be eaten within 3 days. Serve it as it is, or with pasta dishes.

CAPERS
Try to select salted capers which have real flavor. The best are from Pantelleria, Salina, or Lipari. Rinse under cold running water to remove the salt.

CAPRINO
A fresh goats' cheese made with whole or skim milk from the Piedmont region of north Italy.

CARPACCIO
Carpacchio refers to a dish of beef (traditionally) sliced wafer thin. The dish was created by the owner of the legendary Harry's Bar in Venice, Giuseppe Cipriani, in the 1960s. He named the dish after the Venetian painter Carpaccio who used a particular red in his works that reminded Cipriani of this meat. These days the term carpaccio is used to refer to any dish that is served in extremely thin slices.

COTECHINO
This is a soft cured salami from the north of Italy made from the chopped pork meat, fat, and rind. It is sold ready-cooked in vacuum packs. It is served in a traditional dish at Christmas, with lentils and mashed potato.

CRESPELLES
Crespelles are the Italian equivalent of savory crêpes. They can be used instead of lasagne sheets, rolled like cannelloni, folded in fan shapes, or tied as little pouches.

CURED HAM
Prosciutto, cured ham, is the generic name for Italian air-dried ham. Price tends to reflect quality. Opt for either Parma ham or one from San Daniele, sliced very thinly.

DRY, DRYING
To dry cooked spinach thoroughly, put it in a frying pan over a low heat until all the water has evaporated.

EGG PASTA
Unless you can make this yourself, opt for a good-quality (usually described as artisan-made) dry pasta.

GARLIC
Never be without garlic in your kitchen! It is used in countless dishes to flavor oil before sautéing vegetables (and usually removed once the vegetables are cooked).

GREEN OLIVES
Select the fat ones from Cerignola or Lucca or the smaller variety known as picholines.

GORGONZOLA
A blue-veined cheese that can be firm or buttery. It has a salty flavor and plenty of bite. Gorgonzola is very good as it is, with celery. Melted with a little milk or cream it makes an excellent sauce for pasta or gnocchi.

HARD WHEAT PASTA
As with any pasta, artisan-made has the best flavor and texture. Allow 4 cups of water for every 3½ oz of pasta and ½ oz of salt. Follow the instructions for cooking the pasta until just al dente.

LARDO DI COLONNATA
This is the most famous of Italian lard, meaning cured pork fat, from Tuscany. It spends 6 months in marble vats, layered with herbs and spices, to develop flavor.

MARINADE
For Italians, a marinade usually means olive oil, lemon juice, and herbs. Marinating meat or fish imparts flavor and helps to tenderize the flesh.

MASCARPONE
Thick Italian cream made from soured cream, to which buttermilk may be added. It is an essential ingredient of tiramisu, and can be used instead of butter in risotto.

MOSTARDA
A condiment from north Italy made from candied fruit spiced with powdered mustard seed or mustard essence. The most widely available is Mostarda di Cremona.

MOZZARELLA
A white cheese made from either cow's or buffalo's milk (the latter is preferable as it has more flavor). It is usually sold in its own whey or in brine, sometimes vacuum packed. Due to its high water content, it should be used quickly once opened. Serve at room temperature.

OLIVE OIL
Try to buy extra virgin, cold pressed Italian olive oil from the first pressing. As a guide, olive oils from the north of Italy are quite mild, those from the center and the south are more fruity.

OREGANO
Another quintessentially Italian herb. Use the dry variety from southern Italy, preferably organic.

PANCETTA
Rolled dried belly of pork, smoked or unsmoked. It can be used to bard meat, or cubed and added to pasta dishes.

PECORINO ROMANO
A sheep's milk cheese which has a distinctive black rind. It is ideal for shredding over pasta dishes.

PEPPER
Use freshly ground good-quality peppercorns, added sparingly and usually at the end of cooking.

PINE KERNELS
Pine kernels are typical of many southern Italian dishes. The flavor is much enhanced by toasting them first.

PROVOLA (OR SCAMORZA)
A cow's milk cheese which, like mozzarella, has a stringy texture. It is found plain and, for preference, smoked.

REDUCTION OF BALSAMIC VINEGAR
This is balsamic vinegar reduced over a gentle heat to a syrup. You can buy it ready prepared (sold as cream of balsamic) or make it yourself (see recipe 62). It is much used for drizzling over dishes as a garnish and gives a delicious sweet-sour flavor.

RICOTTA
Ricotta means re-cooked. This cheese is made from the whey of cow's or, more often, sheep's milk. It is much used in Italian cooking, in both savory and sweet recipes, particularly from the south.

SPECK
A smoked cured mountain ham, often juniper-flavored.

SUGAR
For desserts, use unrefined cane sugar.

TALEGGIO
A cow's milk cheese from Lombardy. Serve as it is or melted on bruschetta or over risotto, etc.

TINNED OR PRESERVED TUNA
Choose tuna preserved in oil for flavor. Excellent on bruschetta, in salads, pasta, etc.

YEAST
For bread or pizza dough you can buy fresh yeast from a baker. Allow 1 oz of fresh yeast for every 4 cups of flour. Otherwise, buy sachets of dried yeast and follow the instructions for reconstituting it.

MENUS

A formal Italian dinner comprises an aperitif, a starter, an entree (pasta, rice, soup), a main course (meat or fish), and a dessert. For everyday meals, though, a starter and an entree or main course is more usual. In any case, pasta is always present: the reigning monarch at the table!

EXPRESS MENU

Crostini.. 06

Pasta + various sauces.................... 40, 41, 42
Penne with eggplants..............................44
Spaghetti carbonara (without sunchokes)........ 43

Fillet of beef 64
Saltimbocca.......................................66
Baked marinated sea bream 59
Sicilian-style swordfish 58

Sabayon 74
Baked peaches 81

MENU FOR TWO

Salad of raw sunchokes 21

Tagliatelle with mushrooms..................... 34
Linguine with clams............................. 46
Saltimbocca...................................... 66
Baked sea bass with fennel 61
Sicilian-style swordfish 58

Panna cotta 73
Semifreddo...................................... 75

SIMPLE MENU FOR FALL

Crostino with lardo di Colonnata 06

Borlotti bean soup 31
Papardelle with duck sauce 33
Saffron risotto 51

Milan-style osso buco........................... 69
Veal stew with polenta 70

Chocolate amaretti cake......................... 76
Tiramisu.. 72

PICNIC MENU

Sicilian-style pasta salad 48
Bread salad (panzanella)..........................20

Milan-style veal escalopes 65

Sicilian eggplants (caponata)..................... 23
Tomato gratin 25

Baked peaches 81

SUMMER MENU

Bruschetta with tomato 05
Broiled bell peppers 16
Zucchini frittata 28
Stuffed sardines................................ 60

Vegetable stuffed pasta 49
Sicilian-style pasta salad 48
Pasta salad with Sicilian-style pesto 02
Bucatini with sardines 45

Orange & fennel salad.......................... 19
Carpaccio of octopus........................... 57
Veal in tuna sauce 63

Tomato gratin.................................. 25
Sicilian eggplants (caponata).................. 23
Neapolitan-style eggplants 24
Stewed peppers (peperonata)................... 22

Panna cotta 73
Baked peaches 81

WINTER BUFFET MENU

Lingue with pistachio pesto 09
Mini focaccia with olives 11
Breadsticks with lardo di Colonnata & hams... 10

Borlotti bean soup 31
Lasagne verde bolognaise 36
Risotto 50

Veal stew with polenta 70
Chicken & ricotta parcel 67

Oven-baked vegetables 27

Tiramisu 72
Chocolate amaretti cake.......................... 76
Panna cotta 73

MENU FOR THE IN-LAWS

Lingue with sunchoke pesto 09
Mini portions of herb & vegetable pie 29

Asparagus & pea lasagne 37
Spinach & ricotta crêpes 38
Ravioli stuffed with squash...................... 39

Baked sea bass with fennel 61
Guineafowl in pepper sauce 68

Semifreddo 75
Tiramisu 72

CHRISTMAS EVE

Crostini with botargo 06
Lingue with pistachio pesto 09
Mini portions of herb & vegetable pie 29

Carpaccio of octopus on arugula............... 57

Risotto 50
Spinach & ricotta crêpes 38
Linguine with clams 46

Baked sea bass with fennel 61

Rich pandoro dessert 82
Sabayon 74
Semifreddo... 75

BIG MATCH MENU

Pizza (made in advance and
subsequently reheated) 12, 13, 14
Mini fried calzone (deep-fry at half-time) 15

Tiramisu 72
Semifreddo 75

GIRLS' NIGHT IN

Raw sunchoke salad................................ 21
Carpaccio (octopus or beef)............... 57 or 62
Panna cotta 73

CHILD'S BIRTHDAY MENU

Breadsticks with ham 10
Focaccia stuffed with cheese & ham 11
Pizza margarita..................................... 13

Panna cotta 73
Auntie's rice cake 80
Chocolate amaretti cake.......................... 76

CHILDREN'S PARTY!

Herb & vegetable pie 29

Potato or Roman-style gnocchi .... 55 or 56
Pasta gratin 47
Chicken & ricotta parcel.......................... 67

Oven-baked vegetable medley 27

Panna cotta 73

TABLE OF CONTENTS

1

STARTERS

2

VEGETABLES

3

PASTA & CO.

4

FISH

5

MEAT

6

DESSERTS

INDEX OF RECIPES

Note: This index is organized by recipe number.

GENERAL INDEX

Note: This index is organized by recipe number.

ACKNOWLEDGMENTS:

A thousand thanks to all the team involved in this gourmet adventure:
to Pierre Javelle, for his gorgeous photography,
to my assistants: Marie Mersier (styling) and Ariadne Elisseeff (home economist),
to Audrey Génin (project management),
to the publisher Marabout and my editor Rosemarie Di Domenico,
to my friends in Vanves and my daughter Eva!
A big thank you to all those who loaned tools and equipment:
paint, cooking utensils, table settings, kitchen equipment…

For the painted backgrounds:
a big thank you to Pia Jonglez and to Céline from the boutique Ressources:
2–4 avenue du Maine, 75015 Paris, 01 42 22 58 80,
www.ressource-peintures.com

Thanks to the boutique Comptoirs de Carthage for the loan of the crockery
designed by Nelson Sepulveda (manufactured by Belart)
Comptoirs de Carthage: 27 rue de Picardie, 75003 Paris, 01 48 04 37 37
www.comptoirsdecarthage.com

ALESSI: www.alessi.com
BRANDT: www.brandt.com
DRIADE: www.driade.com
GUY DEGRENNE: www.guydegrenne.fr
HABITAT: 0800 01 08 00, www.habitat.co.uk
KENWOOD: www.kenwoodworld.com
KITCHEN BAZAAR: www.kitchenbazaar.com
MATHON 0 892 391 100, www.mathon.fr
MUJI: www.muji.co.uk
PEUGEOT: www.peugeot-moulins.com
PORCELAINES M.P SAMIE: www.porcelainesmpsamie.fr
RIVIERA & BAR: www.riviera-et-bar.fr
ROSENTHAL: www.rosenthal.de
THE CONRAN SHOP: www.conranshop.co.uk
VIREBENT: www.virebent.com
ZWILLING: www.zwilling.com

Props: Marie Mersier
Design: Alexandre Nicolas
English translation and adaptation: JMS Books llp
Layout: cbdesign